THE MELLAH SOCIETY

Chicago Studies in the History of Judaism
William Scott Green and Calvin Goldscheider, Editors

Shlomo Deshen

THE
MELLAH SOCIETY
Jewish Community Life
in Sherifian Morocco

Revised and translated
from the Hebrew by the author

THE UNIVERSITY OF CHICAGO PRESS
Chicago and London

SHLOMO DESHEN is professor of social anthropology at Tel-Aviv University. He is the author of several books on North African immigrants to Israel.

THE UNIVERSITY OF CHICAGO PRESS, CHICAGO 60637
THE UNIVERSITY OF CHICAGO PRESS, LTD., LONDON

© 1989 by Shlomo Deshen
All rights reserved. Published 1989
Printed in the United States of America
98 97 96 95 94 93 92 91 90 89   5 4 3 2 1

∞ The paper used in this publication meets the minimum requirements of the American National Standard for Information Sciences—Permanence of Paper for Printed Library Materials, ANSI Z39.48-1984.

Originally published in Hebrew as *Sibbur vi'yehidim be'maroqo: sidrey hevra biqehillot ha'yehudim ba'me'ot ha'18-19 (Individuals and the Community: Social Life in 18th–19th Moroccan Jewry)*. © Misrad Ha'bitahon, Tel Aviv, 1983.

Library of Congress Cataloging-in-Publication Data

Deshen, Shlomo A.
    [Tsibur yi-yehidim. English]
    The Mellah society : Jewish community life in Sherifian Morocco / Shlomo Deshen ; revised and translated from the Hebrew by the author.
        p.   cm.
    Revised translation of: Tsibur yi-yehidim.
    Bibliography: p.
    Includes index.
    ISBN 0-226-14339-2. ISBN 0-226-14340-6 (pbk.)
    1. Jews—Morocco—Social conditions. 2. Morocco—Ethnic relations. I. Title.
DS135.M8D4713 1989
305.8'924064—dc19   88-27818
                                                              CIP

For
Jacob Katz,
historian of Jewry,
upon reaching the age of 85
in vigor

CONTENTS

Preface ix

Note on Citations xiii

1 Maghrebi Anthropology and Jewish History 1

2 The Political Base: Jewish and Muslim Moroccans 13

3 The Economic Base: Population and Occupations 30

4 Self-Rule I: Individuals and *Negidim* 46

5 Self-Rule II: The Taxation and Charity System 62

6 Self-Rule III: The Sages 70

7 Religious Life: The Synagogues 86

8 Family Life: Individuals among Their Relatives 104

9 Conclusions 119

Notes 125

References 141

Index 147

Illustrations follow page 12.

PREFACE

This study straddles two disciplines, history and social anthropology. It is historical in the sense that the subject matter lies in a past irrevocably gone and that some of the specific topics are discussed diachronically. It is socioanthropological in the sense that other topics are discussed synchronically and that the insight of the theories of anthropologists and sociologists informs it throughout. Also, I identify myself professionally as an anthropologist. Emerging out of a European Holocaust background, I have invested many years in ethnographic fieldwork and research of various kinds among Israelis of North African background, and I pride myself at having, to an extent, "gone native." The present documentary study is partly an off-shoot of that ethnographic work. I have been engaged in it on and off for over a decade, and some years ago published an early version in Hebrew (Deshen 1983), where I elaborated on the impulses that led to this study.

I do not seek here to uncover new documentary sources but rather to systematize information that has been accessible and to present it coherently. While social anthropologists have a predilection for data drawn directly from social actors, preferably by observation, the present study is based on documentary sources. Only marginally, in footnotes and hedged by apologies, have I here and there drawn on insights from anthropological fieldwork on Moroccan Jews.

The documentary sources are rich. They comprise over thirty collections of the legal responsa of rabbis who served in the Jewish community courts of eighteenth- and nineteenth-century Morocco. In these documents we are made privy to the disputes and dramas people brought to court. And while the case material is not as detailed as is the best in field ethnography, it is often vivid and authentic. Frequently the material includes the actual words uttered by people two centuries ago in their strife and predicaments. Written in rabbinical

Hebrew, the responsa were at first collated by the students and descendants of the sages and preserved in family archives. Usually some generations after the death of the authors, the works were brought to press. The earliest of the pertinent tomes was published in Pisa in 1817, and during the nineteenth century other collections were published in Italy. Toward the end of the century many were also printed elsewhere (in Palestine, Poland, Egypt). After World War I, most of the manuscripts were brought to newly established presses in Morocco and occasionally Tunisia, and in our times some are being published in Israel. Another valuable resource that I had at my disposal was the unique archive of the last rabbi of one of the important communities in Morocco, Rabbi David Ovadia of Sefrou. This collection, too, comprising hundreds of private letters and communal documents, has been published (D. Ovadia 1975–1985).

The present study is an attempt to draw out of these sources an overall picture of the society in which the authors of those works lived. I adhere to Goitein's (1974:146) sage view of scholarship as being primarily interpretation, not collation or even edition of information. I have hence made no attempt to incorporate unpublished manuscripts into this study. My ambition is not to present a definitive account, because such an attempt would be precluded by the primitive state of primary archival research in the field of Moroccan Jewry at the present time. My aim is to present a thesis that might stimulate future work, pending examination of the archive holdings (among others the Archive of Jewish History in Jerusalem, the Klagsbald collection in Paris, the Bension collection at the University of Alberta, besides unlisted material in private hands).

Although the basis for the present work is documentary, I have been inspired by my ethnographic fieldwork on North African immigrants to Israel during the years of mass migration. I have also learned from my colleagues who worked in Israel at that time, most of all from Moshe Shokeid who studied a transplanted Atlas Mountains Jewish community. His work, as I specify below, is important, because it confirms independently some of the findings of other Maghrebi area specialists. After the conventional disclaimers about their lack of accountability, etc., for anything that follows, I gratefully mention a few other friends specializing in the field who have also been helpful: Shalom Bar-Asher, Eliezer Bashan, Issachar Ben-Ami, and particularly Rabbi Moshe Amar whose wide knowledge of matters Talmudic and Judeo-Maghrebi is matched only by his modesty. Dale Eickelman,

Norman Stillman, and Walter Zenner read drafts of various sections and versions of the manuscript. Robert Attal, the magnificent bibliographer and librarian of the Ben-Zvi Institute library in Jerusalem, has been of unfailing help for over twenty years. Finally, a word of appreciation to Dorothy Stearn who helped bring the book to press, to Roslyn Langbart and her staff, Pamela Yacobi and Sylvia Weinberg, at the Tel-Aviv University Social Sciences secretarial office, who worked on the longhand drafts. My wife, Hilda Deshen, contributed more than all, and to her the Hebrew version is dedicated.

Besides the aforementioned Hebrew monograph, I have published two papers in English which are partially incorporated in the present work: "Women in the Jewish Family in Pre-Colonial Morocco," *Anthropological Quarterly* 56 (1983): 66–77, in Chapter 8; and "Urban Jews in Sherifian Morocco," *Middle Eastern Studies* 20 (1984): 212–223, in Chapters 2 and 4.

NOTE ON CITATIONS

The pagination of the rabbinical materials that constitute the main sources of this study is often irregular. Therefore, in citing them, after giving the author or editor's surname, I usually refer to numbered sections or items in the works, as is conventional in Judaic studies (thus, Ibn-Sur 137). Where a source collection comprises more than one volume, citation from the first volume is referred to without giving the volume number (thus again, Ibn-Sur 137). Where the citation is from a subsequent volume, the volume number is given (thus, Ibn-Sur, vol. 2, 14). Recurring reference will be made to materials in the first two volumes of the aforementioned David Ovadia collection (1975–1985). In those volumes the document numbers run consecutively. The references therefore omit both volume numbers (thus, Ovadia 630). Sometimes it is necessary to refer to a citation by adding the full given name of the author and the title of a section of the volume (thus, Ya'aqov Berdugo, Even ha'ezer 84). Occasionally the layout of a volume permits convenient reference by page number (thus, Yoseif Berdugo: 80). But sometimes pages have the same number for both sides of the folio. In those cases citation from the first side of the page omits that detail. Where the citation is from the second side of the folio, this is noted (thus, P. Berdugo: 13b). The rabbinical material is still mostly published by private individuals, not by commercial publishers. Therefore the references to the cited materials at the end of the volume do not usually include information about publishers.

In the transliteration of Hebrew phrases, I have let myself be guided by the desire to strike a reasonable balance between approximating the Moroccan-Hebrew pronunciation and not straying far from conventional transliteration practice.

1 MAGHREBI ANTHROPOLOGY AND JEWISH HISTORY

Jewish society in precolonial Morocco presents a paradox. Composed of tightly knit communities, self-reliant individuals also loom large in it. There were to be found in the Moroccan Jewish communities, located usually in secluded quarters, the *mellahs,* a variety of institutions, such as were characteristic of traditional Jewry in most times and places. The social and cultural activities of people in the communities also were largely delimited by the confines of the communities. But mellah society also harbored powerful centrifugal forces, in the guise of the individuals who composed the communities, and who often acted by themselves, oblivious of the formal institutions of the community. Moreover, the sociological structure of the institutions of the communities was, as I shall argue, molded by the centrifugal forces inherent in the communities.

The structure of Moroccan Jewry is characterized by a social script that allows the individual much scope for idiosyncratic choice within the confines of the communal order. Consequently, tension between the collectivism of the community and the particularism of the individual is considerable. The tension between centrifugal forces embedded in the individuals and centripetal forces embedded in the community will recur in the particular studies that compose this monograph. In these studies the focus will be on the various areas of life that engage sociologists, such as economic activities, political organization, religious activities, and family life. The main aim of this monograph is to develop a thesis as to the nature of the tension between individual and community in mellah society, to uncover the relationship prevailing between forces of separation and union. More specifically, I am concerned with questions such as: Where does the community exhibit political potency, and where is it weak? To what extent did people resort to communal institutions, and to what extent did they act upon personal initiative? What was the strength of the

1

family vis-à-vis its individual components and vis-à-vis the larger community?

This study is informed by two approaches that were developed in disparate substantive fields of history and anthropology but hail back to a common source in theoretical sociology. One is the work of Jacob Katz (1961a) on Ashkenazic (Northern European) Jewry of late medieval times, a field basically similar to that of precolonial Moroccan Jewry. Inspired by a Weberian perspective, Katz advanced the study of the social history of Jewry in a much more rigorous way than had been done in the past. Moving beyond issues rooted in the particularities of events, Katz raised new questions about the structure of Ashkenazic society, and he viewed it in terms suited also to the study of other Jewish societies. The effect has been to move the study of the social history of late medieval European Jewry away from parochialism and toward more general mainstream sociological issues.

Another approach that informs the present study is that known as "interpretive anthropology." In the field of Maghrebi studies this has been developed in the past twenty-five years by social and historical anthropologists. These scholars, primarily Clifford Geertz and associates, have uncovered a new image of Moroccan society. From the several major monographs produced by these scholars, there emerges the picture of a society characterized by a powerful individualistic element and a relatively weak corporative element. Bonds of class, tribalism, and religion do not shackle individuals immutably to set positions. Rather, as one representative of this school, Dale Eickelman, put it:

> [In] Morocco *persons* are conceived as the fundamental units of social structure, rather than their attributes or statuses as members of groups. It is the culturally accepted *means* by which persons contract and maintain bonds and obligations with one another which constitute the relatively stable elements of the cultural order. (Eickelman 1985b: 286)

The weight of this insight is compounded by a long-recognized characteristic of Islam in Morocco, namely, the prominence of the element of enthusiastic inspiration relative to the element of ordered, formal, and restrained religiosity. This aspect of Islam in Morocco leads again to an emphasis on the weight of individuals as against that of impersonal institutions, an emphasis that harks back to the Weberian concern with the structure of institutions and their role in society.[1] Of specific pertinence to Judeo-Maghrebi studies is the work of Moshe Shokeid, who discovered in Israel patterns of political behavior that are consistent with the findings of the interpretative anthropologists in Morocco (see Shokeid 1971, and particularly 1979). Although the work of Shmuel N. Eisenstadt is never referred to specifically in the discussions that follow, many of his ideas, particularly of his monumental *The Political Systems of Empires* (1963), hover in the background.

In the present study, I accept the main points of the ethnographic findings of scholars of Maghrebi society concerning the general outlines of the environment in which Moroccan Jewry existed. Further, in focusing on a study of the latter I carry the theoretical concerns that moved Jacob Katz in his study of a comparable society. I seek to broaden the field that engaged previous scholars. Whereas my predecessors engaged in Ashkenazic Jews and Moroccan Muslims, I aim to combine their findings and questions, and add these to the data about Moroccan Jews. This leads me to consider models that might be of direct use in this venture, namely, studies of Jewry in Islamic settings. We have on hand numerous histories, and ethnographies of kinds, of many Jewish societies in the Middle East. The quality of this material, however, is uneven. On the one hand, most Middle Eastern Jewries have been described superficially and upon thin bases of data.[2] On the other hand, one society has been described in a magisterially rich way, Goitein's (1967–1983) "Mediterranean Society" of Jewish merchants in the thirteenth century. Based on the Cairo hoard of manuscripts, "the Geniza," discovered at the end of the last century, the late S. D. Goitein and his associates have in recent years produced voluminous detailed accounts of Jewish daily life under medieval Islam. The weight of Goitein's achievement has not yet been fully assessed in Jewish history or in general Mediterranean studies; the findings have not yet been maturely incorporated into historiography. Consequently, a new pitfall has opened up for the student of Middle Eastern Jewry, namely, the temptation to describe various Jewish societies in Islamic countries according to a model taken from the Geniza materials and "the Geniza society."

In the not-so-distant past, and to an extent today, Middle Eastern Jewish studies suffered from the defects of general Orientalism; the Jewries of "the Orient" were envisioned with Judaic Eurocentric concepts. The questions asked about them were framed by Ashkenazic concerns of the turn-of-the-century variant, with all that this implied in terms of emancipation, nationalism, assimilation, romanticism, and paternalism. Paradoxically, as a result of the great achievement of Geniza Studies, there is now an emerging possibility that Middle Eastern Jewish studies will again be stunted through having a new inappropriate model projected upon them.[3] I consider it, therefore, important to indicate that the society uncovered by the Geniza materials is remote from that which concerns us in this monograph, on two counts. First, "Geniza society" is medieval, prior to the invasions of Central Asian tribes into the Middle East and the ensuing social repercussions (such as the transformation of the Caliphate and the emergence of military empires). Second, a large proportion of the Geniza documents relating to social matters originate from Tunisian Jews, whose Cairo correspondents deposited them in the Geniza (Goitein 1966: chap. 16). This should lead to caution when one is engaged, as in the present work, in a study of Morocco. The Tunisian and Moroccan Jewries are different in early modern times, and one cannot readily assume that in medieval times they were similar.[4]

Our subject is Moroccan Jewry in Sherifian times, and we must now consider its parameters. First, the Jewish element. The delimitation of our study to precolonial times leads us to study Moroccan Jewry as constituted traditionally, before onset of the travails of westernization, secularization, emancipation. In short—traditional Moroccan Jewry, which was a variant of general traditional Jewry. The latter, ever since antiquity, constituted a society, in the sense that it maintained certain common cultural institutions, sometimes also political and economic institutions, that spanned the widely dispersed communities. The fundamentals of Jewish institutions and culture were finally established during the early Middle Ages, when the rabbinical tradition crystallized in the guise of the Talmud, and the Karaite protest against this development floundered and ultimately failed. Ever since, about the turn of the millennium, there has existed a common cultural base for most Jewish communities, and as the Middle Ages proceeded the political and economic conditions of Jews everywhere also came to have much in common. But traditional Jewry evinced many distinct variants. One salient example of such a variant is medieval Spanish Jewry of the so-called Golden Age; another is medieval Rhineland Jewry; a third is Polish Jewry of the sixteenth and seventeenth centuries. These and other such societies, variants of traditional Jewry, differ in the details, but not in the fundamentals, of their social structure and culture, because the existential conditions and historical backgrounds of these societies are basically the same.

In more recent times, on the eve of colonialism in the Middle East and in North Africa, many additional variants of traditional Jewry are discernible. One such variant is that of the Spanish-speaking communities of the Balkans and western Turkey; another is that of the communities of Iraq and Syria. A third variant of traditional Jewry is that of Persia and its satellite communities in Central Asia. Yemenite Jewry is a fourth variant; Tripolitania and southern Tunisia constitute yet a fifth variant. These, and other examples that might be enumerated, represent variants of traditional Jewish society that have consistently different elements of social structure, culture, and customs. Thus, there are indications that the political leadership and family structure of Yemenite Jewry is unique; similarly the pattern of stratification of nineteenth-century Iraqi Jewry is a particular one.[5] The variegation of Jewish societies pertains mainly to details, sometimes nuances, of social structure. The variety needs to be emphasized together with the commonalty. The latter has widely ramified expressions, in religious and in family matters, in communal politics and in social stratification, in relationships vis-à-vis non-Jews and in raising children. But a mature consideration of the nature of particular Jewish societies requires juxtaposition of both commonalty and variety. In the present study we are concerned with the nature of traditional Jewry in its Moroccan guise, the commonalty and variety.

One of the sources of difference between various Jewish societies lies in the variegation of the non-Jewish societies surrounding them. These non-Jewish societies, Muslim, Christian, Hindu—of many kinds and sorts, kaleidoscopically variegated—frequently determine certain activities of the Jews who live among them. Thus the economic activities of Jews are often clearly delimited by rules and customs stemming from their non-Jewish environment. Similarly, the physical security of Jews depends largely upon the doings of non-Jewish potentates (and again Jewish economic activities and relationships with non-Jews are affected). Moreover, disparate characteristics of the various surrounding societies are often linked to elements that are more intimate, internal to the Jewish communities, as I exemplify presently.

Jewish societies, however, are not necessarily influenced, passively and unidirectionally, by their "host societies." Some Jewish societies were long-established in their places, virtually autochthonous, before the currently dominant societies appeared on the scene, while other Jewish societies were migrant newcomers. Jewish societies lived under different conditions that led to disparate experiences of security and insecurity, seclusion or reaching-out, toward the non-Jewish environment. The very term "host society," so often used in discussions of Jewish-Gentile relations, is misleading, because it entails unexamined assumptions of enclosure, inferiority, and alienation in respect to Jewish Diaspora life. I suggest, therefore, that there are parallels between Jewish and non-Jewish living in a given time and place, without implying thereby a determination about the obscure historical sources of peoples' practices. Jews living in any given time and place exhibit a variant of Jewish society, but in their commonalty with contemporary non-Jews they also exhibit a variant of the local society that is common to Jews and non-Jews.

Thus, for instance, there are important parallels between Jewish and non-Jewish social practices in the medieval Rhineland, such as the pietistic movements, the *hasidei ashkenaz* and parallel Christian phenomena (Marcus 1981). There are also similarities in the development of local government of emerging medieval cities and the self-administration of the Rhineland Jewish communities (Baer 1950). Another example is the parallel in certain features of the eighteenth-century Hassidic movement (in the Ukraine) with contemporary Christian sects (Sharot 1982: 145–164). Further, there is the parallel between rationalistic trends in medieval Jewish thought in Muslim lands and contemporary Muslim philosophy. Coming to the field of the present study, I suggest that such also is the case in Sherifian Morocco. While Jews were long-established in Morocco, before the coming of Islam, in time they came to share with Muslims one and the same environment. It is reasonable to assume that some of the social forces that moved people in Morocco were common to all. Thus, while not implying any unidirectional influences, one needs to incorporate the available parallel knowledge about Moroccan Muslims in a study of Moroccan Jews. This confrontation with the Moroccan element in our subject matter leads us to take account of the findings of Maghrebi area studies together with those of Judaic studies.

I move to consider the delineation of time in the subject of precolonial Moroccan Jewry. The main temporal focus of this study is on the 200-year period beginning with the close of the seventeenth-century and concluding with the end of the nineteenth century. I begin with an explanation of the lower time limit. In 1912 the French protectorate was established, and the concurrent change in Muslim power had important ramifications within the Jewish community. Further, in 1918 the colonial authorities legislated a new order for the Jewish communities that signaled drastic changes in self-government and jurisdiction. It is, therefore, out of the question to extend the vitality of traditional society, the thematic focus of this study, beyond that time. There are indications, moreover, that some elements of traditional society, both Muslim and Jewish, already were floundering much earlier. European imperialist incursions were part of the Maghrebi scene during most of the period of our study. The process of the opening of Moroccan coastal cities to Europeans began erratically in the second half of the eighteenth century and became constant in the 1850s. The imperialist incursions had by that time seriously weakened sultanic rule, particularly by the practice of "capitulation agreements." These arrangements, which constricted the scope of Moroccan sovereignty, had ramifications within Moroccan Jewry. They caused a parallel attrition in the authority of the Jewish community over individual community members.[6] In this respect, the year 1894 is a significant marker. Thereafter no sultan arose who maintained any semblance of effective resistance to the encroachments of the European powers.

The development of the French Jewish, modern and largely secular, school network of the Alliance Israélite Universelle (AIU), is part of the process I have indicated. The first AIU schools were founded in the 1860s in Tetuan and Tangier, and by the end of the century such schools were established in most of the large communities. The AIU schools produced graduates who were very different from their elders, and by the turn of the century they had coalesced into groups of AIU alumni. These groups engaged in social and cultural activities, particularly they organized support for their alma mater. The AIU alumni also engaged in philanthropic activities within their local Jewish communities (Laskier 1983:129–130). Although the social weight of the circles of AIU alumni in the communities remains to be assessed more precisely, their appearance on the scene was important and affected the old social structure. Moreover, by the end of the century there also emerged embryonic reformers of another type, literati with a bent for modern Hebrew literary activities (*maskilim*). Influenced by secularized Hebrew-language activists in Europe, the Moroccan Hebrew literati participated in the network of the European Hebrew press and were creative in a new style of Hebrew poetry (see Chetrit 1986; Schroeter 1984a). Both of these new elite circles, the AIU alumni and the Hebrew literati, were active initially in the communities of the coastal regions, where European influence was paramount. But by the 1890s they were to be found also in major inland communities, such as

Meknes and Fez. In view of these developments I suggest a periodization that places the end of the traditional regime in Moroccan Jewry around the 1880s.

The determination of the exact beginning of the period under discussion in this study is more difficult. It is clear, however, that we need not go beyond the late fifteenth century, when Morocco was the haven for many thousands of Jews expelled from Spain, the Sephardim. These refugees settled in the coastal and central regions of the country and soon became dominant elements, even in the ancient major community of Fez. Shortly before the coming of the Sephardim, in 1465, a wave of persecution had swept the Jewry of central Morocco, causing mass defection to Islam and decimating the population. The newcomers thus came to fill vacancies in the ancient communities of the region. Although in the south of the country, particularly in Marrakesh, the autochthonous Jews remained dominant, the Sephardim also came to be influential there.[7] In later sources most of the active voices, particularly of rabbinical and communal leaders, are of people of Sephardic descent. They are known in the sources as *megorashim* (expellees), and the rabbinical figures among them are referred to reverently as *hakhmei qastilia*[8] ("the sages of Castille"). Descendants of the original Jews of Morocco, known as *toshavim* ("the residents"), barely figure among the rabbinical families. Of the major rabbinical families, only the Ibn-Danan family of Fez is of toshavim origin, but even their ancestors lived for some generations in Spain in the late Middle Ages and returned to Fez only in the wake of the expulsion. It is apparent that the authority of pre–fifteenth-century elements, in the communities of central Morocco (and all the more in those of northern Morocco, which were swamped by the Sephardim), fell apart in the course of the sixteenth century.[9] From that time on, most of the communal legislation that has come down to us, and rabbinical writings of other kinds, stem from sages of the megorashim circles and their descendants. Various particular practices of the toshavim were rejected in most parts of Morocco in favor of customs that the newcomers had brought with them from Spain. Once the refugees established their authority Moroccan Jewry became significantly different from what it had been before.[10] The immigration of the Sephardim thus constitutes a sociological turning point.

There are indications that the first two centuries of the period of hegemony of the Sephardim, the sixteenth and the seventeenth, are different from the last two centuries, the eighteenth and the nineteenth. During the first period the communal leaders engaged in considerable communal legislation that has come down to us in the guise of an important codex, the *Seifer ha'taqanot*.[11] Except for that, however, the period exhibits itself as singularly unproductive relative to the vast literary corpus that we have on hand from the people of the later period. I proceed from the premise that the sages of traditional Jewish communities are integral figures in their societies. If then it emerges that the sages of various periods are different, that fact may indicate that also the societies in which they operate are different. And the data on hand, in the case of Moroccan Jewry, point to such a conclusion. Therefore, we cannot remove the beginning of the era of the precolonial society as far back as the sixteenth century.

The Moroccan sages of the sixteenth and seventeenth centuries, besides their codex of abstract legislation, also left a corpus of writings in the area of abstract talmudic discussion, but crucially they left very little by way of responsa on actual matters. They figure as relatively inactive in the explification of *halakha* (religious law) in daily life. Not a single volume of responsa from the early period has been brought to print, and to my knowledge no such volume lies in a manuscript collection. Indeed, isolated documents of the early period do appear scattered in the collections of later writers, but these are quantitatively few. On the other hand the sages of the eighteenth and nineteenth centuries have left dozens of voluminous collections, comprising thousands of responsa. Their creativity is evident in many areas of traditional Jewish scholarly concern: abstract talmudic explification, biblical exegesis, hymn and sermon writing. One might speculate that the difference is just apparent, being caused by the physical loss of the writings of the earlier period. However, the difference in quantity and kind of material on hand is too glaring to dispose of by such an explanation.[12]

Another possible explanation for the difference might lie in the development of Hebrew printing. Ever since the invention of printing, Europe has been studded with Hebrew presses. In Morocco also there was a short-lived Hebrew press established in 1516. Thereafter, no Hebrew works were printed there until the late 1890s, when a press was founded in Tangier. Hebrew printing became firmly established in Morocco only around the 1920s, and from then on the writings of many eighteenth- and nineteenth-century sages came to light (Attal 1980). Crucially, however, also before the reestablishment of Hebrew printing in Morocco in recent times, many works by local sages were printed abroad (primarily in Leghorn, but also in Pisa, Alexandria, and even in Cracow). Therefore, one may deduce that while the lack of a local Hebrew press was a significant factor in the nonpreservation of literary materials, scholars did cope with it. Altogether one ought to bear in mind that voluminous writings of many Jewish sages who lived in times and places just as remote as sixteenth- and seventeenth-century Fez and Meknes have come down to us. If indeed the Moroccan sages of the earlier period had been as prolific as those of the latter period, one might at least have expected to find more mention of them in the later sources. These sources, being of a legal nature, have a natural tendency to seek the precedents of earlier authorities. Therefore, the silence of later sources concerning legal precedents of the sixteenth and seventeenth centuries is significant.

Moreover, we have the case of one particular sage of the early period, Rabbi Yehuda Ibn-Atar (1655–1733), who was particularly venerated in his time and considered the greatest rabbi of his generation. Popularly known as *rabbi el-kebir,* he left behind a number of responsa that his disciples and some sages of later times kept with their own writings. These were eventually published, scattered in the collections of later sages. But comparatively few other early materials were kept in this way. Can one assume that Ibn-Atar's writings in later collections figure there not only because of the particular regard for him, and that also other sages of the seventeenth century were productive? Or, perhaps, Ibn-Atar's contemporaries were less productive and that is why they do not figure in the later collections. Indeed, perhaps the great regard for Ibn-Atar stems precisely from the fact of his superior creativity vis-à-vis that of his contemporaries? The thrust of these considerations leads to the conclusion that the sages of the later period are significantly different from those of the earlier period. A corollary of this conclusion is that the societies of the early and late periods of the era of Sephardic hegemony in Moroccan Jewry constitute distinct variants. Hence I exclude the early period, sixteenth and seventeenth centuries, from the present study, devoted as it is to the precolonial era.[13]

The present study is based primarily on rabbinical responsa from the eighteenth and nineteenth centuries, on the collection of documents published by Rabbi David Ovadia (four volumes on Sefrou and two on Fez), and on the Seifer Ha'taqanot to the extent that it includes late materials. Previous researchers who studied precolonial Moroccan Jewry (Chouraqui 1952; Stillman 1977, 1978; Hirschberg 1981) relied primarily on external sources (travelers' reports and consular files). While valuable data is stored in those sources on matters pertaining to relations between Jews and non-Jews, they do not afford much insight into matters internal to Jewish life. For the latter, we require the testimony of witnesses who spoke the languages and lived the culture of Jews. Further, the external sources do not usually focus upon individual people. To the extent that they do, they highlight individuals who stood out in relation to the extracommunal world, men who excelled in diplomacy and commerce (see Hirschberg 1981: 208–288). Studies based exclusively on the external sources are therefore naturally unbalanced and do not adequately represent the Jewish population as a whole. Many rank-and-file people, however, do figure in the internal sources when their doings warrant the attention of the communal legal authorities. In the rabbinical responsa materials, we are made privy to actual cases of litigation in which we see the sages active in their judicial roles. The cases include disputes between spouses, businessmen, craftsmen, inheritors. Many cases involve the monetary ramifications of marriage contracts and claims involving community taxes and extortions of Muslim potentates. Frequently, the case material includes the actual words uttered by people, frozen, for us to decode and interpret. These data are the closest to field observations that a historically minded anthropologist can hope for.

The usage of rabbinical responsa material is fraught with problems of interpretation (Weinryb 1967; Katz 1960; Haas 1985). Since it is written in the language and terminology of talmudic scholasticism, interpreting the responsa requires specific literary skills. One common pitfall of rabbinical responsa research is the failure to recognize the appearance of stylized literary expressions. Such phrases, while vivid and evocative, may just be vacuous. The responsa are replete with stock phrases, which superficially seem to express particular circumstances of time and place, and apparently constitute grist for the social historian's mill. The writers of responsa, however, are often so immersed in their culture that they have absorbed the turns of phrase and expressions of their antecedents and made them their own without citation of sources. Many phrases and sometimes whole sections of case material are taken from legal and literary precedents. The social historian reading this material must be able to recognize the various historical layers that compose the text. Failing that, one is prone to mistake early materials for later ones. Another common pitfall of research based on rabbinical responsa lies in the casuistic style of this genre of legal writing. The reasoning of Talmudic sages, as they advance toward conclusions, frequently leads them to describe scenarios that could theoretically have arisen in the case discussed. The sages describe ways of action that protagonists could have chosen and other eventualities that could have arisen. Sometimes these scenarios are based on elements of real-life possibilities, but more often they are the products of legal minds that are steeped in Talmudic literature and precedents of other times and places. Insensitive reading of the responsa material sometimes leads researchers to impute reality to casuistic statements that are completely imaginary.

In the past decade a new generation of scholars has arisen which, in line with a newly emphasized interest in the study of Jewry that is not self-consciously focused on relations with non-Jews, concentrates on the internal rabbinical Maghrebi sources. These scholars include people whose often rabbinical and Maghrebi backgrounds serve them well. The present work is part of that wave, but it also brings to the field my own particular background in social anthropology.[14]

The studies composing this monograph open with a focus on the basic conditions of Jewish existence among Muslims in Morocco. Chapter 2 deals with the nature of Islam in Morocco and Moroccan society and with political relations between Muslims and Jews. Chapter 3 deals with the economic base of Jewish existence and describes the material features of the Jewish population and Jewish occupations. The fourth chapter deals with the self-rule of the communities, specifically with lay leadership. The next chapter continues the subject, focusing on the taxation system. The sixth chapter describes the leadership activities of the sages. Chapter 7 deals with religious activities, focusing upon the role of synagogues. The eighth chapter describes family life. A common thread runs through all the discussions of these chapters: the central problematic of Moroccan society, both Jewish and Muslim—the relationship between the authority of the community and that of individuals.

A wealthy nineteenth-century community leader of Mogador (Essaouira). (Israel Museum Collection)

An Amsterdam portrait of the seventeenth-century Rabbi Ya'aqov Sasportas of Salé, who was the foremost opponent of the nascent messianic Sabbatian movement and thereby had a major impact on Jewish history. (Israel Museum Collection)

The Corcos family of the late nineteenth century Mogador (Essaouira), who were one of the wealthiest families of their time and who adopted Western trends, as evinced by their dress. (Israel Museum David Corcos Collection)

A young couple. (Israel Museum Collection)

Utensils for the serving of tea in an affluent Fez Jewish home. (Israel Museum Collection)

Ladies in an affluent home in Erfoud. (Israel Museum Collection)

A shopkeeper studying while waiting for customers. (Israel Museum Ivor Schwartz Collection)

A Marrakesh merchant and a Muslim customer. (Israel Museum Ivor Schwartz Collection)

A textile merchant studying while waiting for customers. (Israel Museum Collection)

Rabbis of Fez, Meknes, and Sefrou in the 1930s. Second from right is Rabbi Yedidia Monsoniego (the present chief rabbi of Fez and all Morocco). Fourth from right is Rabbi Yoseif Meshash (figures in Chap. 2). First from left is Rabbi David Ovadia (compiler of the Ovadia collection and presently living in Jerusalem). (Israel Museum Collection)

The florid signatures of eighteenth- and nineteenth-century sages, among them that of Rabbi Eliyahu Sarfati (figures in Chaps. 4 and 5). (Israel Museum David Ovadia Collection)

An example of calligraphy and fine manuscript production: an eighteenth-century prayer book. (Israel Museum Collection)

A teacher with his students in Tiznit. (Israel Museum Collection)

Synagogue chanting: one of the main expressions of religious and artistic creativity
of Moroccan Jewry. (Israel Museum Collection)

Rabbi Refael Anqawe of Salé (d. 1935), a prominent rabbi of late precolonial times.

Rabbi Barukh Toledano, the last Meknes sage of the distinguished Toledano lineage, pictured in the 1970s in Israel. Many rulings of the Meknes Toledanos figure in text.

The fine interior of an affluent Jewish home in Fez. (Beth Hatefutsoth, the Nahum Goldman Museum of the Jewish Diaspora)

2 THE POLITICAL BASE: JEWISH AND MUSLIM MOROCCANS

Jews in Morocco lived within the confines of a Moroccan Muslim environment, and an outline of that environment follows. Ever since medieval times, Moroccan Islam stands out by its vitality. Some of the most zealous, aggressive, Islamic revitalization movements of all times stemmed from Morocco. Thus, the Almohads surged out of twelfth-century southern Morocco to spread throughout Northern Africa and the Iberian peninsula. The Islamic movements asserted themselves both by their political and religious fervor, and the intensity of their campaigns left a permanent stamp on the history of the western Mediterranean. From these movements emerged ruling dynasties whose center was usually in Fez, the ancient royal city graced with distinguished religiocultural institutions. The source of power of the rulers of Fez, however, often lay in the tribal people of the Atlas Mountains hinterland and in the religious impulses that moved those people. The Atlas Mountains potentates, many of them Berbers, thus laid their own tribal stamp on the cities of Morocco and on the Moroccan political system.[1]

The tribes were potent in large regions of northern and central Morocco that fringed on the mountain areas, particularly in the mountain areas themselves, and in the southern part of the country. Tribal potentates were influential also in the cities of those regions, including the royal cities of Fez and Marrakesh. Urban strata, such as those developed in many other parts of the Middle East, were weak in Morocco until well into modern times. While the cities were to a considerable extent composed of extensions of tribal formations, the nonurban regions were not characterized by a strong locally rooted peasantry but rather by transhument sheepherders. The country was thus weak in both urban and peasant elements.

This general social structure of Morocco was paralleled by particular features of medieval Moroccan Islam. Although the cities boasted venerable mosque-universities, such as the Qarawiyin in Fez and the Yu-sufiya in Marrakesh, the *ulama,* urban sages vested in Islamic law, were not the paramount religious leaders. That role was filled primarily by marabouts (*murabetin*)—enthusiastic, inspired, holy men who were be-lieved, as their title implied, to be bound up, shackled, anchored in the deity. In contrast to the restrained, dignified, and aloof ulama, the marabouts fired the popular religious imagination. The believers saw in their person a vessel of potent holiness that exudes *baraka,* bountiful blessing and potent fertility, to those in the saints' ambience. Accord-ing to popular religious conceptions, holiness is predicated upon en-thusiastic morality, total personal loyalty, and exceptional physical prowess and personal charm. The believers felt that this combination of traits was an expression of the supernatural, the holy and godly. And, remarkably, people believed that marabout holiness in the form of baraka could be transferred to others by contact with the physical person of the holy man. The political predominance of tribes, to a large extent transhument, is paralleled by an enthusiastic, charis-matic, religious leadership. The element of stable institutionalized strata, based on frozen, clearly defined vested interests, either material or cultural, is thus relatively not very potent in traditional Morocco.

The forces of tribal and marabout power increased in time. The Berber dynasties of the thirteenth and fourteenth centuries managed to retain power for periods that extended over several generations (be-fore being overthrown and replaced by a new wave of political insur-gency from the Atlas Mountains hinterland). But by the late fifteenth century the tempo of insurgence and changes of potentates increased dramatically. The role of marabout charismatic leaders in politics be-came constant, and as a result sultanic rule disintegrated completely by the sixteenth century. During this period, known among historians as *la crise maraboutique,* a new element became significantly prominent in Moroccan Islam, the claim of noble descent from the Prophet, being of *sherifi* lineage. Individual marabouts adopted noble patronyms, and this led whole sections of tribes to change their names. Soon the claim-ants for power asserted themselves not only on the basis of their per-sonal charisma but also on the basis of putative prophetic lineages.

The innovation was an expression of the depth of the maraboutic crisis.[2] People were faced with a bewildering dilemma: they had to choose between numerous political pretenders who supported their claims with both purported religious inspiration and florid genealo-gies. Moreover, there was no escape now from deciding upon the ram-

ifications of the basic problem: Of the numerous members of the retinue of a given marabout, to whom does one attribute baraka, potency,
and authority similar to that of the master? The new element of lineage
in marabout identity, newly developed after the sixteenth century, was
both an expression of the crisis of political legitimacy and an attempt
to resolve it. The element of lineage constituted an attempt to insti-
tutionalize political leadership and mute its individualistic charismatic
element. But in practice this was no solution, for the number of claim-
ants of sherifi lineage simply multiplied.

In the middle of the sixteenth century, however, a dynasty (apparently of Berber origin) from the Tafilalt region, on the fringes of the
desert, mustered the military force to hold on to the sultanate for
several decades. Later, in the seventeenth century, the phenomenon
recurred, and the new dynasty, the 'Alawi, managed to retain the sultanate. In fact, its descendants fill the role of sultan to this day. The
'Alawi, therefore, warrant particular attention since they were the sultans under whom the Jews of precolonial times lived the longest period. The 'Alawi sultans do not claim merely to be direct descendants
of the Prophet. Styling themselves as Commander of the Faithful (*amir
al-mu'minin*), they claim thereby to be epitomes of those who carry the
mantle of the Prophet. This powerful claim for legitimacy, backed by
effective use of the military and political instruments at their disposal,
has been a major base for the remarkable longevity of the 'Alawi dynasty.

The 'Alawi sultan's legitimization upon the most characteristic sym-
bol of Muslim authority, that of being Commander of the Faithful, the
political heirs of the Prophet, was a double-edged sword. On the one
hand, it did indeed powerfully legitimize their rule vis-à-vis anyone
who dared oppose them. But, on the other hand, this very legitimization exposed the sultans to religious criticism and potential control.
Whereas a ruler who is devoid of religious pretension is not expected
to act in religiously approved ways, one who claims to be the Commander of the Faithful naturally opens himself to scrutiny according
to the rules of stringent morality and religion. Indeed, over the centuries, the 'Alawi sultans were time and again engaged by insurgent
tribes who, impassioned by marabouts, found fault with them as Muslim monarchs.[3]

The implication of these developments for Islam in Morocco is the
crystallization of institutionalized charisma, as expressed in the political role of the 'Alawi sultan. However, another important social role,

that of the ulama, fares very differently under the circumstances of
Sherifian Morocco. The ulama are of secondary importance only, vis-à-
vis both the sultan and the marabouts. It is the latter by their inspired
exhortations who, directly or through intermediaries, evaluate the actions of the sultan. But the ulama, whose expertise it is to evaluate
actions by the practice of reasoned and sober confrontation of actuality
with religiolegal texts, are an altogether weak element.[4] The effect of
this is that abstract law is only a secondary base for the legitimization
of sultanic authority, while the element of personal religious loyalty to
the Commander of the Faithful is the primary base. The ramifications
of this state of affairs can be traced in widely disparate areas of life and
in the administration of state affairs. The Sherifian state had barely any
bureaucracy that could serve as an independent organ through which
the sultan could exercise his policies. Further, the state lacked an educational, welfare, or legal system of its own. It also had no effective
control of any religious body. Crucially, Sherifian Morocco lacked a
state mechanism to obtain revenue from taxation. And the ultimate
was that the sultan generally did not have command of substantial
armed forces. Those forces which the sultan did command usually
amounted to no more than a glorified bodyguard; for serious strategic
requirements he needed to have recourse to sources beyond the control
of the state. Yet the Sherifian empire maintained itself vis-à-vis grave
external challenges for hundreds of years and never succumbed totally
to external powers. The 'Alawi dynasty actually outlived the era of
imperialism. How was this achieved?

Sultanic authority entailed primarily face-to-face interaction between the sultan, or persons of his immediate entourage, and his subjects. To the extent that the sultan maintained such interaction the
potential of his authority usually became translated into power.[5]
Where, however, the arm of the sultan did not reach, his authority
remained vacuous, authority devoid of power. Thus the sultan typically obtained taxes from the various regions of the country by presenting himself there in person. These visitations took the form of
grand colorful processes (*harka*). The monarch, with a vast entourage
of hundreds, sometimes thousands, of armed and unarmed retainers,
guards, and valets, would make grand appearances and extort his dues.
The armed forces, however, were those of tribal groups who subordinated themselves to the sultan. Such groups, when loyal, followed him
and acted on his behalf against dissident groups. The sultan thus
maintained the contours of the territory under his effective rule, the

blad al-makhzan ("land of the treasury"), which otherwise might, imperceptibly and easily, drift into the *blad e-siba* ("land of dissidence"), where his rule was only theoretical and ineffective.

The conceptual distinction of the two kinds of territory reflects the nature of the Moroccan polity. It was far from the insubordinate Berber tribes of "the land of dissidence" to repudiate in principle the authority of the sultan, the Commander of the Faithful. It was only at times when the sultan did not exert actual power and physical presence over his subjects that the latter acted as sovereigns in practice. There was no stable boundary between the blad al-makhzan and blad e-siba. The one constantly drifted into the other, depending upon the monarch's ability to impose his authority upon his subjects, either in person or through a close representative.

The first 'Alawi rulers made an attempt to create a political and administrative base for themselves by establishing a new capital. They developed the town of Meknes and moved the court there from the royal city of Fez. But the attempt failed, and the new capital soon became just another royal city in addition to the older ones (Fez and Marrakesh). The sultanic practice in reference to the new capital fell into the groove of traditional practice. Instead of the sultan ruling over his domains from his Meknes base, there developed the practice of royal processes (*harka*), the mobile court that moved between the royal cities and demonstrated the power-laden presence, political and religious, of the Commander of the Faithful.

During the nineteenth century the imperialist powers encroached increasingly upon the sultanic domains and obtained domination over various sectors of the population and over certain spheres of activity. The most overt expressions of this were the extension of foreign citizenship to native dignitaries and the dumping of cheap imported manufactured goods on the local market. These developments had ramifications beyond the people immediately affected, and they greatly increased the old pressures on the central polity. Consequently, the nineteenth-century sultans resorted to the harka measure to assert themselves. We have on hand several vivid accounts of harkas, particularly of the last one of Sultan Mulay Hasan (Harris 1921: 10–14, also 54–64), during which he died in 1894. The sultan had been ailing but nevertheless proceeded on his months'-long journey, attended by a huge retinue of courtiers, servants, and guards. When the sultan died, the courtiers feared that the potentates of the regions the caravan was due to pass through would revolt. They therefore dressed the corpse up and presented it as if alive in the royal carriage. And thus, encouraging motions of obeisance from the populace they passed, the cortege traveled for several weeks, in the oppressive summer heat, with the decomposing body of Mulay Hasan regally seated. Only after the harka was completed was the sultan buried.

From the seventeenth century on, Islam in Morocco is thus focused increasingly on individual personalities whose power is rooted in their inspiration and excellence and increases to the extent that they claim descent from the Prophet. Conversely, religious authority stemming from investiture in law decreases. In Fez and Marrakesh there indeed continued to operate the ancient mosque-universities that host ulama scholars learned in Islamic law. By the eve of the era of colonialism, however, their power, relative to that of other Moroccan religious potentates, was one of the weakest in Muslim lands. This reality has many ramifications, beginning with the status of the sultan and on to many details of daily practice in matters such as folk worship at the purported graves of holy men. The vitality of Islam in Morocco also has ramifications in the area of relationships between Jews and Muslims. At this point, then, we turn to a discussion of the development of these relationships against the particular background of local religious and political conditions.

Through the Middle Ages, both under Christianity and Islam, people did not have rights as citizens but rather as members of the particular strata to which they belonged. Their rights differed according to the differential political, economic, and religious power of each stratum. These conditions also pertained to Morocco and Moroccan Jewry until the onset of colonialism. People's rights depended on the extent of their power. Jews in Morocco, indeed throughout Muslim lands, lacked power of any kind, physical or political. Jews were tolerated, "protected" in medieval parlance, and therefore they were not required to convert to Islam. However, the discriminatory charter of the minorities, the *dhimmi*,[6] applied to them. According to the dhimmi charter, the believers were obliged to subordinate the infidels and their religions. The subordination had many expressions. One was the prohibition of building new places of worship. Another was the prohibition against wearing shoes in public, especially near mosques. There were prohibitions against wearing fine clothing and against riding horses. Jews were required to yield to Muslims in public thoroughfares. They were forbidden from holding street processions (hence the custom in many localities of disturbing Jewish funeral processions), and so forth. The spirit of the dhimmi charter is to create a wide gap between the honor due to Islam and the faithful and the status of the tolerated religions and of their adherents. The exercise of physical, military, or political power is an intrinsic component of the honor that is rightly due to the believers only. The exercise of such power by Jews, and certainly its legitimization, is an affront to Islam and is prohibited outright. Beyond this negation in principle of Jewish power, Jews were usually powerless also in actuality, but that was not always so. During the Middle Ages, as the caliphate disintegrated and the military regimes were establishing themselves, many Jews throughout Islam earned fame as senior administrators of Muslim monarchs. In Morocco during the eighteenth and nineteenth centuries, there were no such glaring contradictions between theory and practice. At most, Jews rose to positions of diplomacy, acting as middlemen between the Sherifian empire and European powers. These positions were side activities of traditional Jewish commercial activities; they did not entail independent positions of power. In Moroccan society, composed primarily of militarily powerful tribes, the Jews were vulnerable and exposed as merchants and craftsmen.

The major Jewish communities of our period were located in the main cities such as Fez, Meknes, Marrakesh, and Tetuan, which lay mostly within the confines of the blad al-makhzan, the domain under the immediate and personal authority of the sultan. But even there the sultan did not usually have the support of a supratribal force of his own. He often relied on his ability to command obedience through the power of his baraka, the charismatic power-laden spirituality of his being the Commander of the Faithful, descended from the Prophet. Lacking overpowering material coercive force, an important expression of the sultan's authority lay in the extent of the peace and order that prevailed in the cities of the blad al-makhzan. The security of urban Jews, the weakest and most exposed of the sultan's subjects, was an important manifestation of sultanic power. Attacking the Jews of the cities who were close to the sultan was an affront to the sovereign. A chronicler of the late eighteenth century, in praising the powerful sovereign of an earlier day, expresses this well: in those times, "even a woman or dhimmi could travel from Oujda to Wadi Nul" unmolested (cited in Stillman 1977). During unruly periods when sultanic power was weak, the monarchs were particularly sensitive to the political implications of harassment of the Jews. The scenario reported by a Fez chronicler of an insurgence in the 1790s is characteristic. The rebels, who overran the city, assailed the local Jews by beginning to build a mosque in the Jewish quarter. Thereupon the Jews appealed to the sultan, and he ordered the structure to be dismantled (Ovadia 1979: 73). In order to limit the exposure of Jews to insurgents and thereby to advertise their own impotence, the sultans enclosed Jewish communities within the confines of the walls of their quarter, the mellah.[7] This confinement was viewed by the Jews as "a sudden and bitter exile" (cited in Stillman 1979b: 80, and n. 55); and it was probably partially motivated by the desire to isolate and ostracize the Jews. Spatial seclusion in the mellahs was also aimed at the physical protection of the Jews, albeit for political and not altruistic reasons. Notably, it lacked the predominant discriminatory motives, religious and social in nature, that motivated European rulers in their times to restrict Jews to ghettos. It is characteristic that seclusion in many of the major Moroccan mellahs, such as Marrakesh, Salé, Rabat, Tetuan, and Demnat, were rigorously reimposed on Jews during the nineteenth century, at a time when sultanic power was beleaguered by the advances of imperialism and the subsequent extortion of capitulation agreements (see Schroeter 1982, in reference to the community of Essaouira specifically). During the late seventeenth century and parts of the eighteenth century, however, when sultanic power was at its height, comparatively little is heard of confining Jews within mellah walls.

Nevertheless, even during quiet periods, sultanic protection was not sufficient to free the Jews from harassment. The reason for this is rooted in the nature of the Jewish economy. A study of nineteenth-century lists of Jewish occupations reveals that over one-half of male urban Jews earned their living by traveling for extended periods in tribal areas away from the cities (Chap. 3, below). The tribesmen of those regions, both Arabs and Berbers, although not necessarily denying the sovereignty of the sultan, usually behaved independently, being bound only by the rule of local potentates. The economic activities of lone travelers, particularly of unarmed and despised Jews, were possible only if formal and stable arrangements had been effected with the tribal chieftains. Thus it is seen that Jewish economic activities were dependent on sultanic protection within the cities, and on tribal protection in other areas.

The two kinds of protective ties complemented each other. Sultanic protection tended to be communal in nature. It encompassed an entire mellah community, providing security for urban Jews, including the

women and children whose menfolk were absent. Tribal protection, on
the other hand, tended to be individual in nature. It was extended to
the individual Jew who required protection in a particular, idiosyn-
cratically defined area. Because of individual economic connections
with certain tribesmen, each Jew, or each small group of partners,
required a unique network of patrons that provided security along each
particular route. And since tribesmen often controlled only short
stretches of a route, the individual merchant (on his behalf only or on
behalf of a small number of partners) perforce had to make arrangements with numerous potentates. The Jews who lived away from the
royal cities were helped little by sultanic protection. They in particular
required individual arrangements. The account of an anthropologist
(Rosen 1972), who studied the town of Sefrou (on the fringes of the
Atlas Mountains, southeast of Fez) in the 1960s, depicts Sefrou Jewry
as a community whose security depended mainly on the personal ties
of individuals. Another anthropologist (Shokeid 1982), who studied a
community of Jews from the Atlas Mountains now resettled in Israel,
came to a similar conclusion.[8]

The rabbinical sources are replete with incidents concerning Jewish
peddlers and craftsmen who were killed by robbers while traveling.
The most common fear of travelers, however, seems to have been not
loss of life but rather loss of property. This fear is well demonstrated
in the general statement of a nineteenth-century Tafilalt sage: "We see
that when [highwaymen] set out to rob, their intention is to take
goods and to capture Jews, and hold them till they get redeemed"
(Abihsera 75). Jews extricated themselves from such situations by activating ties with patrons. Such ties were often ramified, beyond monetary payments. Frequently they included handicraft and business services that continued for a lifetime; sometimes these even passed from
one generation to the next. In this manner, patron-client relations
were bolstered by family tradition, feelings of loyalty and trust. Occasionally, there was also a sacral element to these ties, such as when
they were forged by 'ar, an oath and animal sacrifice at the doorstep of
the Muslim patron (Westermarck 1926: 518–569; Brown 1982; Jamous 1981: 213–216; for the operation of 'ar seen from the Jewish
angle see Ovadia 55). The principle guiding the 'ar was that an important personage brought shame upon himself if he refused a request
made by a person of lower status making a sacrifice on his doorstep.
This placed the weak in a position of manipulating, of virtually forcing
the powerful. All this led to a situation where molesting a Jewish

client infringed upon the sphere of influence of the Muslim patron of that client.

Although we do not know definitely to what extent the mechanisms of patron-client relationships afforded security, I suggest that individual ties were more effective than communal ones. This contention is supported by the fact that in the rabbinical sources there are numerous reports of urban Jews being attacked violently with loss of life, whereas from remote Tafilalt we have the mild statement recorded above which conveys a less insecure situation. There are also theoretical considerations that would lead us to expect that sultanic protection, the only protection available to sedentary Jews, would be far from fully effective. First, city Jews, although protected by the sultan, were natural targets for insurgents who aimed at the sultan. Second, the cities were arenas for the learned activities of Islamic scholars, the ulama. Those, by their very being, reminded the sultan of his religious duties as Commander of the Faithful, and these duties had clear, negative implications vis-à-vis the Jewish position.

The patron-client relationship between a Muslim potentate and his individual Jew had many facets. It was both harshly authoritative and affectively friendly. On the latter plane we find mutual visiting on family festivities, and even participation in a whole range of ritual activities. These included visiting saintly graves, mostly Jewish but also Muslim, hallowed in common by both Jews and Muslims, and prayers of Jews and Muslims during times of drought.[9] One of these ritual activities, the Mimuna Jewish folk festival, has been closely studied (Goldberg 1978). Muslims filled an important role in this festival by providing the first leavened food after the Passover festival, when Jews refrain from such food. The Jewish Mimuna festival thus functionally required the participation of Muslims. Some of the cases recorded in the rabbinical responsa reflect a loyalty and devotion between individuals that cross-cut the ethnoreligious divide. We learn of the practice of eighteenth-century Meknes Jews who, when threatened by insurgents, gave their valuables for safekeeping to Muslim acquaintances (R. Berdugo 1891: 264). A nineteenth-century Sefrou source reports a case in which two Jews who were clients of different Muslim patrons owed money to each other. The source relates that the creditor did not pursue his case. He was apprehensive lest the dispute lead to violence between the Muslim patrons, and he feared that his patron's life might be endangered (Ovadia 319). An eighteenth-century Meknes source reports an incident in which a local Muslim potentate visited a Jewish home together with a Jewish visitor. During the course of the visit the Jewish visitor asks the Muslim to arrange a match for him with the host's daughter (H. Toledano 156; see also Ibn-Sur 18). The note of intimacy is striking and extended to the sensitive context of marital affairs.[10] From eighteenth-century Tafilalt, in the south, we hear of the complaint of a synagogue cantor

> that when he used to officiate we did not respond "Amen" to him.
> So he went to the daughter of the king, and complained, "Your Highness, the congregation does not respond 'Amen' after me!" Thereupon she immediately sent her servants, and they beat us. Then we called out "Amen" loudly after the cantor. (Cited in an unpublished dissertation by Bar-Asher 1981: 106)

Again the intervention of Muslim potentates in profoundly internal Jewish matters, albeit of clear sociopolitical import, is salient.

Moving to consider the view that the Jews had of their neighbors, a starting point is the research of Jacob Katz (1961b), on relationships between Jews and Gentiles in Ashkenazic Jewry of the seventeenth and eighteenth centuries. Katz presents the Ashkenazic sources as being replete with expressions of revulsion vis-à-vis Christians and Christianity. Ashkenazic Jews felt the symbols of the alien religion as being diffusely fearful and profoundly defiling, virtually demonic; they tried to avoid them as much as they could. Against that background the sources of Moroccan Jewry presented a great contrast. The religion of their Muslim neighbors did not concern the mellah people very much. Further, the scant indications of concern that the sources do contain do not show evidence of feelings of the kind that have been documented for Ashkenazic Jews. Rather than disgust and repulsion, among Moroccan Jews the sources reflect contempt and disregard. The mellah people engaged Islam in a very different way from that of their contemporaries under Christendom. Thus, in Fez in 1688 there came before the local sages a perennial issue of internal taxation, the question of exemption of scholars from paying community taxes. On principle, such exemption was accepted virtually everywhere in Jewry, but in practice it aroused recurring disputes. The Fez court upheld the principle of exemption once again, but it offered a supporting argument that is illuminating in our context.

> Even gentiles, whose laws (*datoteihem*) are all stolen from the true and just law (*dat ha'emet ve'hasedeq*), respect their prayer leaders, priests and scribes. (Seifer ha'taqanot 148)

Therefore, the court went on, Jews most certainly ought to show respect to their own dignitaries and absolve them of taxation. In this context the alien system is not reviled. More, it is remarkable that the Jewish sages mention non-Jewish dignitaries in terms of a reference group and suggest their position as a parallel for the problem on hand. Their feeling is one of disregard for the religion of the environment, based on the conception that Islam is insignificant because it lacks originality.[11] But where contemporary Ashkenazic Jews would flee from Christianity in horror, the Fez sages do not evince particular discomfort facing the religion of the non-Jews in their environment.

Ashkenazic Jews in premodern times were naturally apprehensive and suspicious of interreligious dialogues. Among Moroccan Jews there are some indications of discussions and of interest on the part of Jews about the religion of their neighbors. In the hagiography of Rabbi Ya'aqov Abihsera (1807–1889) of Tafilalt there are several mentions of religious discussions the sage purportedly held with Muslims (Moghrabi 1968: 59–66, 155–156; see also Stahl 1980). The legendary context of those accounts precludes the separation of fact from fiction, but even if the accounts are only fictional it is their popular recounting that is significant. From a somewhat later period we have a startling autobiographic account of the Meknes sage Rabbi Yoseif Meshash (1891–1975). As a youth, he writes, he visited Malaga in Spain, for medical treatment, and chanced upon a Catholic priest near his church. The two engaged in conversation (in Hebrew), and the priest invited the young man to see his church. Meshash accepted but stipulated, "Without taking off the hat!" (Y. Meshash 1970: 133). From the context of the account it appears that the sage had never seen a church before; his personal experience of non-Jewish religion was limited to Islam, and he infused that into the novel situation in which he found himself. The outcome was one of aroused curiosity, which the sage did not stifle but rather filled in a manner that was consistent with his notions of religious pride. It is significant that the sage recounts the incident many decades later in his memoirs. The behavior described thus emerges as reasoned and deliberate and not as youthful idiosyncracy. It is hard to conceive a comparable Ashkenazic sage acting similarly at any of the stages of the incident.

Another text, pertinent to the elucidation of interfaith relationships from the Jewish angle, is appended to the collection of legal responsa of an early nineteenth-century Meknes sage. The latter recounts a lengthy conversation that he had "with a Gentile, one of their wise men (*piqheihem*),[12] who was honorable and desired to learn the truth." The conversation consists of standard Muslim challenges toward Judaism, such as figure in the religious and philosophical disputes of medieval times, and of equally standard Jewish responses (Perlmann 1974; also Stillman 1979a: 65–68, and refs.). At the end of the discussion the Jew challenges Islam (in the spirit we saw above in the Seifer Ha'taqanot source). The author concludes that his adversary was unable to respond to those challenges, and "he took leave of me with an unhappy countenance and disturbed spirit (*panim sehubot ve'leiv hamarmar*)" (P. Berdugo 42). The story is phrased in exuberant triumphant terms, but there is no evidence of repugnance and disgust in facing the alien religion. Altogether, the style of the account is not customary in rabbinic writing, and one may raise questions as to the reality of the story.[13] Be that as it may, the account as such, and the fact of its preservation and eventual publication in a collection of responsa, reflect a particular attitude toward the religion of the environment, namely, that Islam is deemed to be a partner worthy of debate, in a way that was common at the height of the Middle Ages.

The last rabbi of Sefrou, Rabbi David Ovadia (b. 1913), recounts a remarkable tradition about one of his nineteenth-century predecessors, Rabbi Refael Moshe Elbaz (1823–1897), that indicates how comfortable the two religions could be with each other. Ovadia (1975–1985, vol. 4, Toledot: 67) writes:

> [During times of famine] the great one of the Muslims used to ask him to pray much . . . for they regarded him as an angel. And sometimes, when the Imam used to ascend the tower of their house of prayer at dawn to welcome the day with songs of prayer, the rabbi also used to respond to him (*oneh liqrato*) from the window of his home with hymns (*baqashot*) in Arabic. The Imam [then] used to be silent to hear him.

As in the previous case, the authenticity of the incident is not certain. The significant point is the fact of the account.

The sources lead to the conclusion that the attitude of the mellah people to the religion of their surroundings had two components. There was an element of disdain and superiority but also an element of openness and debate. There is no evidence of the characteristically Ashkenazic attitude of horror and disgust toward Christianity. The view of Islam among Moroccan Jews is linked to the status of Judaism in Islam as against the status of Judaism in Christianity. Christian theology nurtures a convoluted obsessive fascination with Judaism, which harks back to the Church fathers and the foundation of Christianity. The history of Islam, being very different, has no comparable concern with Judaism. Islamic belief is obsessive only on one specific issue: its superior status vis-à-vis the inferior status of all other religions. Stillman (1977) summarizes:

> There is no obsession with the Jews comparable to that found in mediaeval European literature. Most of the Moroccan stereotypes of Jews may be negative, but they are also peripheral. They are perceived primarily as dhimmis, humbled, but protected subjects. As long as the Jew conforms to this role, he arouses little interest.

Jews are not particularly salient in the Muslim view and do not consume much of the theological energy of Islam.

When, however, Muslim sages do direct their attention to Jewish matters their attitude is basically inimical (see Stillman 1979a; Friedman 1979, for Islam in general; and Stillman 1977, 1978, for Morocco in particular). Moreover, the aforementioned obsession of Islam is not unique regarding its relationship toward Judaism but toward all religions. Within that universal category, Judaism shares with Christianity the favored status of dhimmi, toleration (which, as we have seen, also implies subordination as a matter of course). In many Muslim lands (but not in Morocco), there are both Christian and Jewish minorities, therefore Judaism does not usually fill a unique niche in Muslim thought and life.

The view of Judaism entertained by Islam is paralleled by the view of Islam entertained by Judaism that we saw above, namely, aloof disdain. Although in the Middle Ages there was theological grappling with Islam on the part of Jewish philosophers, the ultimate and prevailing view of the latter was that Islam was not worthy of serious engagement. They believed that whatever positive features Islam had were to be found also in Judaism. When a religion is perceived in such terms it does not constitute a formidable opponent nor, alternatively, a monster to be battled against or to be avoided at all costs. Theologically, Islam was not the abomination to traditional Judaism that many other religions were. This had important ramifications. In times of stress people might be driven to convert to Islam, and they could rationalize that move by arguing that this was not apostasy to a serious rival, certainly not to an idolatrous creed. The reactions of Jews under

Islam were thus very different from those under Christianity. Jews under Islam might convert temporarily or permanently, because they had fewer inhibitions toward Islam than their parallels had toward Christianity.[14] The important sociological effect of this attitude was to make mellah society relatively permeable to external social forces.

The features of the non-Jewish environment, both those general to Islam and those peculiar to Morocco, had ramifications in the structure of the autonomy of Moroccan Jewish communities. In particular, the personal dyadic ties between Muslim patrons and Jewish clients were important. These ties cross-cut internal ties within the Jewish community, sometimes obstructing communal loyalty. Their overall effect was to impede the operation of communal institutions and of Jewish autonomy in general. The community often had individual members who were independent of community authority and institutions. Moroccan Jewish community leaders, like their peers in other Jewish societies in traditional times, sought to maintain asymmetric relationships with the local gentile authorities. The Jewish community endeavored to limit the sphere of influence of the gentile authorities. Particularly in matters of litigation between members of the community, the Jewish authorities insisted on the exclusive jurisdiction of Jewish courts of law; individual recourse to gentile courts of law was regarded as a heinous sin.

The Jewish communities themselves, however, routinely had recourse to gentile authorities in cases of litigation against powerful Jewish individuals. In such instances, the Jewish authorities needed the legal and political backing of the gentile authorities. Also, since the Jewish authorities usually lacked executive power such as a penal system, gentile assistance was required to execute the law as adjudicated by Jewish courts. The asymmetry of the relationship lay in the fact that the Jewish authorities prohibited individuals from involving gentile authorities in internal Jewish affairs but assumed for themselves, as corporate bodies, the prerogative of obtaining assistance from the gentile potentates and their courts of law. This asymmetric relationship, and the attempts to maintain it under diaspora conditions, was one of the basic problems of Jewish autonomy. The asymmetry was never consistent, and Jewish communal autonomy was therefore not impervious to interference, both by gentiles from the outside and by powerful members of the community from inside the community.

In Sherifian Morocco, in particular, the asymmetric relationship vis-à-vis the Muslim authorities was far from perfect. Despite repeated prohibitions on the part of the sages we find numerous instances of individuals turning to the gentile authorities and to their courts of law. We also encounter Muslim authorities intervening with the Jewish authorities and the Jewish courts, in favor of particular Jewish clients. Also lay community leaders could not be sure that their deliberations remained private, nor that internal matters would not be leaked to the Muslim patrons of individual community leaders. In an eighteenth-century Sefrou source the following is said about the secrecy of communal deliberations vis-à-vis Muslim potentates:

> No one can say a thing against their will, or do anything about it, because they are so fearsome. . . . Everything is overheard and the wall has ears. (Ovadia 21)

There are many accounts of individuals who evaded communal taxation by activating the protection of their Muslim patrons. Thus, according to an eighteenth-century Fez source:

> Many people get assistance from the lords of the land and procure for themselves documents of exemption. Some people free themselves of all taxes; others arrange to pay a little—just as they please. (Ibn-Sur 22; see also M. Toledano: 57b; Yoseif Berdugo I, 1922–1943, vol. 3: 34b)

We hear of legal cases in which Muslim potentates intervene in the Jewish court on behalf of their clients; also of litigants who evade the Jewish court in preference for a Muslim court where their patron wields influence (Ovadia 97, 368). We read about a Jewish court that could not operate because a litigant failed to present himself before it "because he is a Jew of the enemies" (H. Toledano 237). The man was a client of a Muslim patron who was quarreling with the potentate of the area in which the court was located.[15] The prevalence of patron-client relations between individual Muslims and Jews in that case stymied the operation of the Jewish court. In another case we encounter the ultimate development of such conditions—the Jewish court positively recommending to a plaintiff that he have recourse to a Muslim court of law (Yoseif Berdugo I, 1922–1943, vol. 2: 29). We also hear of a Muslim patron intervening in the divorce proceedings of a husband seeking to evade payments that he owed his wife (Ovadia 97). Further, we encounter marital cases where the courts are strongly pressured by litigants supported by Muslim potentates (Mordekhay Berdugo: 62; Ben-Malka: 87b).

Muslim influence penetrated the community in yet another manner, through people whose business affairs were limited or nonexistent and who had no influential Muslim patrons. These people, often destitute and reduced to begging, nevertheless had a potent resource that enabled them to pressure the Jewish authorities: the threat of defecting from the community and converting to Islam. Such threats were particularly voiced in connection with taxation problems and debts. Individuals unable to cope with exorbitant extortions of Muslim potentates, as mediated by the Jewish community authorities, sought to escape their lot by converting (Ibn-Sur 202; Ovadia 97). In times of unusual material pressure, the Fez chronicles recount, numerous people relieved themselves of the burden of belonging to the humiliated highly taxed dhimmi stratum by converting to Islam (Chap. 3 below).

The permeability of the Moroccan Jewish community had another facet: the relatively weak institutionalization of various community organizations—political organs in particular. While this, as I have indicated, is a universal Jewish problem, there are differences in detail between various Jewish societies. Certain communities, particularly in the Ashkenazic orbit and in medieval Spain, enclosed themselves more effectively from external potentates than did the communities of precolonial Morocco. In the chapters that follow, on the autonomy of the community, we will examine the means by which Jewish community heads sought to secure asymmetry of access to external potentates and to govern. We shall see that the structure of social relationships, both between Jews and Muslims and among the Jews themselves, frequently permitted access of one and all in the community to the sources of power, thus obviating asymmetry.

3 THE ECONOMIC BASE: POPULATION AND OCCUPATIONS

The major Jewish communities of Morocco during the eighteenth and nineteenth centuries were to be found in the north and center of the country. In the south, except for Marrakesh and Essaouira, the communities were relatively small, and they were culturally less creative than those of the north. Wars and natural disasters recurrently struck the country. Periods of famine resulting from drought, and epidemics aggravated by poor sanitation, were common. Sometimes people were plagued by floods or swarms of locusts. All these misfortunes instilled in people feelings of insecurity and fear for their welfare, and particularly for the lives of their infants. Indicative of this is the standard blessing given in the synagogue to an individual who has participated in the Sabbath Torah reading—that "the Lord keep his children safe." But the blessing was not always fulfilled, and infant mortality was very common.[1]

The frequent disasters caused significant loss of population in the communities. While the historical sources do not express these losses in quantitative terms, they are nevertheless eloquent. Thus Moroccan Jewry (following upon the ruling of Sephardic sages) permitted polygamy under two conditions: that the existing marriage was childless, and that it had been maintained for ten years.[2] In the sources of our period, we find cases of childless individuals pleading for permission to marry second wives before the elapse of the ten-year period. The reasoning appended to these pleas is illuminating. Summarizing one of them, Ibn-Sur writes: "In these five years . . . [the plaintiff] has seen all the members of his family die of hunger and plague." In pleading for permission to marry a second wife after only five years of childlessness, the man hoped that "perhaps he will become rebuilt through her" (Ibn-Sur 22). Another sage, Rabbi Hayim Toledano of Meknes, writes about a case where the plaintiff argued that "no mortal can know when his time will come, and he alone remained from the family of his father's house." The plaintiff had noted that Toledano's late father, who had also been a judge in Meknes,

> used to exert himself to overrule (*mistaer le'vateil*) this regulation about the ten year period, and particularly in times of famine such as these, where several families had been obliterated, and only scattered individuals remained. (H. Toledano 51)

Normally Moroccan sages greatly respect "the regulations of the megorashim," of which the one under discussion is a part. Here, remarkably, a ruling of the revered ancients is being directly overruled. The issue indeed seems to require the sophisticated manipulation of the judge by this knowledgeable plaintiff by reminding the judge of his father's position.

It barely needs saying that the quantitative data we have on hand are thin. For eighteenth-century Moroccan Jewry there is nothing approaching reliable statistics, but for the second half of the nineteenth century, and particularly for the end of the traditional era and the beginning of colonialism, we do have some data. Michael Laskier, who has marshaled many late nineteenth-century sources, comes to a concluding estimate that the total Jewish population of Morocco amounted to about 100,000 people (Laskier 1983: 21–22). The largest late nineteenth-century community was probably that of Marrakesh, for which there is an 1867 report of 6,000 individuals; the population is reported to have risen to 14,000 in 1902, and to 16,000 in 1906 (Deverdun 1959, vol. 2: 562). Fez, the next largest community, is reported as follows: 9,000 in 1877 (Laskier 1983), 5,844 in 1879 (Le Tourneau 1965: 307), 15,000 in 1882 (Laskier 1983). On the eve of conquest the varying figure given is 10,000 (Laskier 1983) and 8,000 (Le Tourneau 1965: 19). Schroeter (1984b: 50) determines that in 1875 the Jews of Essaouira numbered about 7,000, having increased from 4,000 in 1844. For Sefrou we have a late nineteenth-century report that there were in the community 750 working-age men (Ovadia 135). That figure indicates a total population of all demographic categories that would be at least three or four times as large, namely, around 2,500. However, Rosen (1984: 14) marshals figures to the effect that in 1883 the Jews of the town numbered 1,000, and 3,000 in 1903. Other communities for which large figures are cited are: Meknes, 6,000 in 1901 (Chouraqui 1952: 222–223); Tangier, 5,000, and Mazagan, 3,000, both in 1873 (Laskier 1983).

Coming to comparative data with earlier periods, we naturally tread uncertainly. But we do have some indications on hand. For Sefrou we have the estimate of Ovadia that around 1770 there were "at least 450 families" (Ovadia 1975–1985, vol. 3: 112). This figure is not exactly comparable with the figure Ovadia cites for the late nineteenth century because there were probably more working-age men than there were heads of families. Due to the young age of marriage, however, the numerical difference between the two categories cannot have been very great. The Fez estimates appear to be quite erratic, but the Essaouira, Marrakesh, and Sefrou figures do indicate an increase in population in Moroccan Jewry in the nineteenth century. The conclusion that there was some demographic increase, I shall argue, is of major sociological import.

The urban communities of nineteenth-century Morocco were large by the standards of community size of traditional Jewry. The leading communities of comparable Jewish societies, such as those of Northern European Jewry in the eighteenth century (that is, prior to the dramatic increase in population that took place thereafter), were usually not larger, and many were smaller. Also in the Muslim orbit only a few communities, such as Salonika and Baghdad, stand out as being substantially larger than Fez and Marrakesh. In terms of Jewish sociology, the leading Moroccan communities constitute large populations, and even a community such as Sefrou should not be seen as a small one. The people who comprised these communities lived in great congestion in the mellahs, the Jewish quarters, into which most of the communities were enclosed by the early nineteenth century.

The occupations and livelihood of the people of these communities were determined by the general conditions prevailing in the country. The social structure of Morocco was permeated by the dichotomy of cities, on the one hand, and dispersed tribes, on the other. Beyond that there were relatively few centers of population, such as villages and towns, that served as commercial centers mediating between the cities and the tribes. Consequently, the Jewish city dwellers developed a pattern of peddling that entailed moving directly from the major centers deep into the tribal hinterland. Although the peddlers often remained away from their homes for weeks and months, they did not move their families to the region where they made their living because they favored city life and were strongly attached to their home towns. The movement of a vast sector of Jewish menfolk among their Muslim clients, spatially far from their home communities, is a factor of major demographic and social importance in the overall situation of pre-colonial Moroccan Jewry.

We have on hand from the late nineteenth century data about two important communities of central Morocco, Meknes and Sefrou, that permit an insight into details of their occupational structure. The two localities were very different in terms of urbanism and economy. Sefrou was a provincial town whose overall population in 1883 is given as 3,000 (Rosen 1984). In sources of the early eighteenth century it is sometimes called "a village." Meknes, in contrast, was a royal city, raised to that status in the late seventeenth century. While we lack a precisely comparable figure for the Meknes population, it was doubtless much larger than that of Sefrou. In the eighteenth-century Jewish sources the Meknes community is frequently mentioned jointly with that of Fez, in contexts implying that both are equally important.[3] Ecologically the localities of Meknes and Sefrou are very different. Sefrou lies at the foothills of the Atlas Mountains eighty kilometers east of Meknes, and it maintained close social and economic relations with the transhument Berber tribes of the hinterland who engaged in shepherding. Meknes, on the other hand, lies in the Sais plain, a different ecological and economic environment. It was a relatively sophisticated urban center, home to many potentates and grandees close to the sultan. Meknes is at the core of the blad al-makhzan, whereas Sefrou lies at its fuzzy fringes.

Despite these differences in the general setting, it is remarkable that the Jews of Meknes and Sefrou had important economic features in common. The Meknes source informs us that the community was composed in 1901 of 1,137 families totaling 6,000 people (Chouraqui 1952: 223–224). The number of working-age men probably exceeded that figure, for despite the young marriage age some men in the labor force were still unmarried. My present purpose is to arrive at a picture of the relative occupational spread of people, without attempting to obtain absolute numbers. Therefore I proceed on the assumption that 1,137 heads of families constituted the labor force of Meknes Jewry. The source further reports that about 400 men were engaged in four crafts—button making, tailoring, sandal manufacturing, and silversmithing (listed according to their size). These occupations have a clear common denominator. They are typical of a class that services the needs of a well-to-do urban population. The source mentions no other specific occupation, only claiming that besides the categories mentioned there was "a mass of peddlers." Both the categories of the craftsmen and the residual one of peddlers doubtlessly included both poor and well-to-do (who paid taxes and maintained the community institutions). The salient difference between the categories is, primarily I suggest, not in their relative wealth but rather in their overt mode of occupation. The aforementioned crafts, being orientated to the needs of the local grandees, led to a sedentary way of life. The craftsmen did not need to move out of the town (in fact, it is not conceivable that the manufacturers of fancy buttons, tailors, and so forth, could make a living among the coarse tribesmen). The "mass of peddlers," on the other hand, engaged in purveying manufactured goods the tribesmen required in the countryside and also imported the products of the tribal economy into the city. The peddlers thus engaged in a highly mobile life, spending much time away from the city in the countryside. The following important point emerges from the data: a large sector of the population of Meknes Jewry, numbering many hundreds of men, moved as individuals among the Muslims, away from their community and families.

The Sefrou figure that is pertinent for purposes of comparison is that of 750 adult men cited by Ovadia (135) for the late nineteenth century. While this reflects a much larger population than the one reported by Rosen, our interest at this point lies not in establishing absolute statistics but rather in uncovering the relative distribution of occupational categories. From that point of view, the Chouraqui and Ovadia data for Meknes and Sefrou, respectively, are comparable. The Sefrou report states that out of 750 men there were 110 craftsmen engaged mainly in leather making, metal working, soap manufacture, woodwork, and building. The overall profile that emerges from this list of crafts is one of craftsmen who are close to the products and needs of the Berber shepherds who come to the town. With the possible exception of the soap makers, these are craftsmen who are geared not to serve an affluent urban population but rather a tribal population that requires basic needs for livelihood (such as metal implements) and the means to market their products (such as facilities for processing sheep hides).

The Sefrou source also mentions eighty merchants who engage in importing and marketing out of permanent stores in the local market, and also in extending loans to agriculturalists. This category of businessmen, presumably well-to-do, included men whose occupations led them to sedentary lives within the Sefrou market confines. But there were also many who, due to the close ties with the Berber economy, must have moved frequently among the tribesmen, financing productive activities, sometimes contracting partnerships with the tribesmen. It is reasonable to assume that these conditions often made it necessary for prosperous Jewish merchants to travel into the hinterland and spend time away from their homes.

The Sefrou source reports a third category of breadwinners—thirty sages, who lived off tuition fees, the income of synagogues and endowments. In later chapters we shall consider the livelihood of sages in detail. The salient point in the present context is that the sages, together with members of the two previous categories (the craftsmen and the merchants), a total of 220 men, constituted a relatively sedentary element in the Sefrou economy. Despite the qualifications that I have indicated, these were people whose livelihood essentially came from their store, workshop, or synagogue.

Crucially, however, in Sefrou as in Meknes, there was a large residual category of people who, lacking a local economic base, were perforce in constant movement. We hear of 300 men engaged in peddling in the surroundings of the town, and of 250 who are described as poor and beggars. Many of the latter presumably maintained a precarious existence by offering their menial services to affluent townsmen. But many roamed far and wide, trying to peddle their wares or to obtain some chance work from the tribesmen. The latter two categories, of peddlers and beggars, numbering 550 men, thus include many hundreds of people whose material conditions led them to a life of perpetual movement, away from the community. One gains the impression that this category of people was somewhat larger in Sefrou than in Meknes. Given the differences of opportunity between a provincial backwater and a royal capital, that is only to be expected. The larger and more affluent market of Meknes offered more scope for the Jewish merchants. Moreover, as we shall see below, people entertained a bias in favor of sedentary livelihood, and to some extent the city afforded that more than did the town. The crucial point of the analysis, however, is that despite the differences of detail, the category of spatially mobile individuals is very large, in both Meknes and Sefrou.

We have on hand the reports of contemporary ethnographers: Geertz, Geertz, and Rosen (1979) on Sefrou, and Eickelman (1983) on Boujad in the Tadla plain. The conclusions of their studies lend support to the thesis that the above findings have an element of generality beyond the two communities that I have discussed. According to these ethnographers, the traditional Jewish economy was characteristically orientated toward the tribesmen. Both studies conclude independently that at the end of the colonial period about 60 percent of the Jewish merchants engaged in trade with tribesmen, beyond the confines of the towns. On the other hand, the ethnographers report that only about 20 percent of the Muslim merchants engaged in this kind of trade. The Muslim merchants concentrated primarily on the local urban clientele. Eickelman and Geertz found no other significant difference between the Muslim and Jewish merchants. They indicate, in particular, that neither Muslim nor Jewish merchants specialized in any particular type of goods. It is the concentration of Jewish merchants upon a particular category of clients that struck them as noteworthy. Income from the Berber trade was lower than from the local market; also, it was more arduous, sometimes dangerous. Given the overall setting of the Jewish merchants as dhimmi among dominant Muslims, this division of labor is linked to ethnoreligious specialization and discrimination common in the Jewish condition. The Muslim merchants established themselves in the more lucrative niches of trade and drove the Jews to peripheral, less desirable ones. The trade specialization in the present case, however, has a uniquely Moroccan aspect.

In many places and times, occupational discrimination has led to the concentration of Jews in certain trades (particularly tanning and metalworking under Islam, and moneylending under Christianity). Islam, however, has no tradition of an antimercantile prejudice, and in Morocco in particular many Muslims were merchants. Islam is concerned primarily with the issue of the relative status of various religioethnic groups, and that concern in particular informs the Jewish economy under Islam. Jews were driven into a type of trade that entailed a particular kind of social relationship. Trade with tribesmen necessitated moving into the villages and residential encampments of the clients and business partners. Particularly, it necessitated entering the privacy of homes and doing business with women. Such contacts are highly problematic among Muslims. The men responsible for Muslim women (husbands, fathers, or brothers) are profoundly shamed by the intrusion of males into the domestic orbit of their womenfolk, and the women for their part are suspected of promiscuity. Muslim men are therefore inhibited from establishing any kind of contact with Muslim women that is not mediated by the male guardians of the latter. The occupation of peddling, however, requires contact between the itinerant dealer and whoever happens to be home at the time of the peddler's visit. The Muslim norms thus effectively prohibit Muslims from engaging in peddling and limit them to the fixed marketplace. Jewish males, on the other hand, being despised and deprived of respectability, are not considered sexually dangerous. Since Muslim women are therefore not considered vulnerable to Jewish peddlers, their entry into the female orbit is not an affront to Muslim honor (Jamous 1981: 68).

We have on hand a third set of data on precolonial Jewish occupations, from Fez (Le Tourneau 1965: 100), that is comparable to those of Meknes and Sefrou. In Fez, in contrast to the other communities, we encounter the phenomenon of markedly more craftsmen and fewer merchants. Le Tourneau reports that on the eve of the establishment of the protectorate there were 8,000 Jews in Fez. If we now assume an average family to be composed of five people (see Chap. 8 below for elaboration), there were about 1,600 families in Fez, a figure that is presumably somewhat lower than that of working-age men. Le Tourneau now reports that no less than 600 men worked as silversmiths and goldsmiths. He also states, without giving figures, that many Jews worked as weavers. From a study of the eighteenth-century occupations of Fez Jewry (Bentov 1966), we know that the community nurtured a rich tradition in the crafts. People also worked in crafts other than those mentioned in the Le Tourneau list. Thus we can deduce that out of 1,600 workingmen, many hundreds, perhaps close to a thousand, were craftsmen. Relatively, then, the category of merchants and peddlers, although it comprised hundreds of men, was smaller than that of the communities of Meknes and Sefrou.

An attempt at explaining this finding requires consideration of certain aspects that are peculiar to the background of Fez Jewry. Lying between Meknes and Sefrou, the ancient capital harbored the largest Jewish community of central Morocco. It was graced by the presence of some of the greatest Jewish luminaries of all times (such as the twelfth-century Maimonides who lived there as a young man, and his predecessor, the halakhic codifier, Rabbi Yishaq Alfasi). After the expulsion of Jews from Spain in 1492, many of "the sages of Castille" settled in Fez. The city was, however, also a major center of Muslim religiosity and learning. The local ulama took care that the discriminatory laws concerning the dhimmi were carried out in practice in their vicinity. The ulama also closely scrutinized the doings of local potentates in this matter. One result of the presence of many learned Muslim clerics in Fez was the recurrent and severe pressure, effected time and again upon the Jewish community. We have on hand numerous accounts of waves of persecution in medieval times that led to mass conversions. David Corcos (1976: 28–29) reports that even in our times one encounters among old Fez Muslim families many erstwhile Jewish names and that there are traditions of old Jewish origin among them. Incidents of persecution leading to conversion also figure in the sources of the sixteenth to eighteenth centuries. The purported quantitative dimensions of the conversions are astonishing. The chronicles of the Ibn-Danan family recount that 600 people converted in 1606, and soon thereafter another 2,000 converted. In 1724 1,000 Jews are said to have converted (Ovadia 1979: 1–4).[4] Also Ibn-Sur (33) mentions conversions in the early years of the eighteenth century.

The conversion figures cited in the chronicles are probably grossly exaggerated, for the whole Fez community amounted to only a few thousand people. If indeed conversion was as massive a phenomenon as is claimed by the chronicles, one would have expected a complete disintegration of the community. However, with the exception of the persecutions of 1465 which affected the community very seriously, the sources do not offer any evidence to that effect. Given this reservation on the data, they do indicate that defection from the Jewish community was not just a matter of idiosyncratic individuals but rather one of significant social dimensions.

Though painful and regretted, defection was considered part of life. The feelings of people of the eighteenth century about the incidence of conversion are well reflected in a case that involved a broken contract of betrothal. The father of a bride had broken an agreement that he had contracted with the father of a young man after he discovered that the groom "had become an informer both covertly and overtly." The father of the groom now sued for damages, but the court dismissed the claim on the following remarkable grounds:

> Although some time ago, before the betrothal [the] brother [of the groom] converted, and nevertheless [the plaintiff] agreed to the match with his daughter, that does not warrant that he should also suffer this ugly blemish. For in these times conversions are common, and people do not refrain from marrying [the kin of converts]. But this great blemish—the ears of all that hear it tingle! (M. Toledano: 30)

The salient point is that conversion is viewed with relative mildness because it occurred in so many families. While such families were presumably considered tainted, the source indicates that other families nevertheless intermarried with them.[5]

I suggest that the occupational spread of Fez Jewry is linked to the background that we have seen. Large groups of the old community had, over the centuries, removed themselves into the Muslim milieu. Since their motivation was linked to persecution, we may reasonably assume that upon conversion these people improved their material condition. In terms of commerce, the converts must have sought to escape hazardous peddling in exchange for safer and more lucrative sedentary business in the local market. On the other hand, in a situation where the occupations of Jews are scrutinized in terms of the dhimmi compact, such as they were in Fez under the wrathful eyes of the ulama, the Jews are prone to be driven into occupations that are specifically earmarked for them, such as metalworking. These factors, I suggest, explain the comparatively low representation of Fez Jews in commerce and the comparatively high one in the crafts.

The many differences between Fez, Meknes, and Sefrou—ecological, political, cultural—led to differences in the details of Jewish occupational distribution in the various communities. Crucially, however, beyond these relatively minor differences, a major common element looms large: the fact that in all the communities there was a vast population that did not make a living in a sedentary fashion. In each of the communities hundreds of men moved over distances, peddling goods or selling their skills as craftsmen, away from their hometowns. Seen against the backdrop of the great social contrast between the three localities—Fez, a proud cultural and political center; Meknes, an upcoming political center; Sefrou, a provincial backwater—the commonalty of the Jewish occupations stands out. Many Jews perforce were driven to travel distances as the only means of making a living. They saw their condition as unfortunate. The traditional Middle East altogether maintains a bias favoring urban life, and Jewish Middle Eastern culture reflects this. One powerful Jewish expression of the urban bias is the common text of grace recited after meals according to the Sephardic custom. When people are hosted by others, they commonly invoke blessings upon the master of the house. This routinely recited text reads as follows:

> May the Merciful One bless the master of this house . . . with
> sons who will live and belongings that will multiply . . . and
> may his and our belongings be successful and close to the city.

In Morocco, specifically, leaving the confines of the hometown and the city generally was considered unfortunate. The responsa of our period are replete with evidence as to the very tangible dangers involved in interurban travel. Many of the legal discussions involve incidents of peddlers who lost their lives due to violent attacks by highwaymen. Sometimes the peddlers disappeared without leaving a trace, and sometimes the identification of bodies of slain peddlers was dubious. Such events led the surviving spouses of the unfortunates to become classified as *aguna* (pl. *agunot*), women of unclear marital status, and objects of halakhic attention (hence the documentation in our sources). Other halakhic discussions involve the loss of property caused by highway robbery, particularly when these losses impinge upon problems of partnership, liability of third parties, and inheritances.

Despite these dangers, many individuals traveled great distances. In particular during the spring and summer months, after the Passover festival, many peddlers absented themselves from their homes, sometimes for weeks and months on end. One source speaks as a matter of course that on the Sabbath the community does not get together in the synagogues because many people are away among the Berbers (Yoseif Berdugo II: 170). Many more people absented themselves from the community for the duration of the working week and returned home for the Sabbath (Ovadia 1975–1985, vol. 3: 126, and the sources cited; M. Toledano: 42). People were loath to leave their hometown. A striking testimony is that of the father of a poor scholar, who lived off charity that he collected traveling from one Jewish community to the next. The father writes a letter of anguish to his son, begging him not to travel too far:

> [Please] travel in the direction of the town of L'ksabi where people know us, and surely their gift to you will be large. That is better than to go to places where we are unknown. Every night I raise my eyes to Heaven and beg of God that He should not take you out of your place, that He supply your needs in your hometown. (Ovadia 501)

Characteristically, the writer of this letter does not grieve as much over the fact that his son is reduced to begging as he grieves over the fact that he does so among strangers.

Together with the universal attraction of life in the hometown, the mellah people had a distaste for life in small and distant localities, away from the large communities. This is frequently expressed in marital litigations, when husbands try to impose upon their wives a shift in family residence to hinterland localities closer to their source of livelihood than their home communities, and their wives object. Such opposition on the part of wives is an important source of the phenomenon of workingmen traveling long distances to make a living. The courts routinely supported the wives in these disputes, arguing that a husband does not have the right to move his wife from her familiar surroundings against her will because of his problems in making a living.

The sages in particular had reservations, sometimes crude prejudices about their coreligionists who chose to live in small localities. They suspected such people of seeking to evade the control of the Jewish authorities, for instance, by taking a second wife under improper conditions. The dearth of scholars in the hinterland caused the sages of the large communities to fear that people would contract legally flawed marriages and divorces and thereby arouse problems of marital status (see Ya'aqov Berdugo, Even ha'ezer 51, 52, 62). Describing the qualities of a man living in the hinterland, whose reliability as a witness he was assessing, a sage gives free rein to his prejudices:

> I have seen that he is unqualified, because he is one of those villagers who does not know his right from his left [hand] . . . a complete boor (*am ha'ares mi'deorayta*) who does not even know an *aleph,* but rather a *beheima* (beast) in the form of a *gamal* (camel), one of the stones of the field (*avnei ha'sadeh*),[6] an animal! (A. Anqawe 75)

The text evinces a wordplay that is typical of Hebrew writing of the times. The writer plays upon the first four letters of the Hebrew alphabet, hinging upon them uncomplimentary rustic images. The form of the play determines much of the content of the text, so it would be inappropriate to take its meaning literally. Nevertheless, it is clear that prejudice and animosity permitted this literary play.

People nurtured strong feelings of local patriotism toward their communities, and of prejudice vis-à-vis neighboring communities and the people living there. Thus a Sefrou woman in a letter (probably dictated by her) concerning the selection of a bride for her unmarried son, objects to "one who is sly like the Fez women" (Ovadia 401). The negative image of the women of the neighboring community emerges in the course of the flow of the message; nothing that was said before warranted the reference. But for the writer it seems to have been a natural way of clarifying her meaning, although the Jews of Fez and Sefrou maintained friendly contact with each other. And in times of trouble people of one community regularly sought refuge among those of the other.

Moreover, people were inhibited when there arose the issue of shifting residence between the two closely related communities of Sefrou and Fez (Ovadia 440). We also encounter Sefrou preachers, when castigating their flock, playing upon feelings of local patriotism. Expounding on people's laxity in a matter of ritual observance, a local preacher harangued his congregation:

> Visitors who come from Fez and Meknes are astounded at this forbidden doing among us, in this town of sages. (Ovadia 274)

Such feelings also figure in the sages' private correspondence. In a letter written by a Sefrou father to his son, apparently a somewhat frivolous teenager who was spending time in Fez, we read:

> How terrible! What will the Fez Jews say of you?! They will say "Come and see that man's son, going wild and dissolute . . ." They will say "Shame on the Jews of Sefrou!" (Ovadia 299)

And Meknes and Fez sages castigate the people of Sefrou as follows:

> Don't spoil the reputation of the whole of your community, God forbid! For you have a good name, praise to God, throughout the Maghreb, because the people of the Sefrou community are charitable . . . and abide by [the teaching] of sages. (Ovadia 9; also vol. 4, 37).

Even a Sefrou individual who eventually made his home in Fez, and in fact expressed himself satisfied there, continues to think in communal terms. He writes back to his hometown:

> Praised be the Lord! The Jews of the community of our town [who live] here are all honored. They all earn well, praised be the Lord. And I am one of them. (Ovadia 8)

We thus encounter the argument of local patriotism in a variety of social contexts, and in all of them people evidently considered it to be persuasive.

The physically mobile element in the community comprised the peddlers and also many merchants and craftsmen, besides occasional professional beggars—altogether a vast sector of the population. In contrast to the physically mobile, there was a sedentary element, people more or less riveted to their places of work in the towns. These included many of the well-to-do merchants of the market, many craftsmen, and the sages who offered legal, religious, and educational services. We hear of craftsmen who, far from operating individually among the tribesmen, cooperated and maintained close ties among themselves in the towns. The evidence comes particularly from Fez (Bentov 1966; Elbaum 1972: 28), and indicates the existence of a guild-type situation, familiar to us both from the Christian and the Muslim Middle Ages. We hear of an association of Jewish silversmiths, who jointly took upon themselves the responsibility of paying any fines or extortions that the authorities might impose upon individual members (M. Toledano: 59). We also hear of an association of tailors that processed the materials supplied to it by the monarch for the needs of his court. The association became involved in litigation, because some of its members apparently produced shoddy work, and the others, fearing they all might suffer from the wrath of the authorities, preemptively sued their colleagues before the Jewish court (Ibn-Sur, vol. 2, 119). Similarly, we learn that five ritual slaughterers in one locality cooperated: all the income of their work was gathered in a common fund and later divided among them according to a fixed formula of percentage (Ovadia 1975–1985, vol. 4, 160).

We do not know to what extent employed labor was common in the communities. It probably was not, because people mostly learned their trade from their fathers and naturally moved into family enterprises. However, due to the misfortunes of early deaths, it is probable that young boys were often driven to hire themselves out into apprenticeship. A Sefrou employment contract has come down to us that details the terms of a young apprentice in soap manufacture. He was obliged to work without limit, as demanded by the employer; in return the latter was to house and feed the apprentice as if he were a family member. The employer had to supply the apprentice with shoes; he also had to pay an agreed sum one-half year after the end of the term of employment (Ovadia 162).

A corollary of such diffuse agreements between individual employees and employers was the prohibition, incumbent upon employees, from associating in unions against their employers (S. Y. Abitbul 60). The relationship was one of multiplex ties, beyond specific labor ties. Also, the relationship between a craftsman and his client had a similar multiplex quality. From a Meknes case we learn of local Jewish barbers who made a living from permanent clients. One day, we are told, "a man [left] his craft and wanted to be a barber. He went out and enticed the customers of the old [barbers]." The sage, Rabbi Refael Berdugo, ruled against the man (R. Berdugo 1891, pt. 2, 33). The judgment implies that the relationship of craftsman and client was a stable one that did not permit free economic competition. From the same sage we have another pertinent ruling. Berdugo adjudicated a case where a group of craftsmen (we are not informed which craft) sought to enact a regulation that would be binding on all members of that particular craft in the community. That, the sage declared, was illegal (R. Berdugo 1891, pt. 2, 31). The juxtaposition of these two cases is illuminating. It indicates the parameters of the associative tie of craftsmanship, as conceived by one particular sage. According to R. Berdugo the element of craftsmanship is binding among people, to the extent that ties with a client are conceived of as binding, and may not be broken by economic competition. But, on the other hand, craftsmanship does not constitute a commonalty that permits the foisting of unwilling associations and regulation.

Whatever the force of the occupational bonds that existed within the Jewish community, it must always be seen within the context of powerful centrifugal forces, bonds that linked Jewish breadwinners with Muslims beyond the Jewish community. Toward the end of the era of tradition, during the second half of the nineteenth century, there emerged new extracommunal bonds that intensified the existing situation. The new developments are ramifications of the incursions of imperialistic powers into the Sherifian empire. The capitulation agreements that were granted by the sultan, particularly after the 1850s, permitted the European powers to maintain agents, who were legally answerable to them and not to the authorities of the land. Many local entrepreneurs, among whom Jews figured prominently, thus obtained the citizenship of European powers and became subject to the jurisdiction of their respective consuls only. In terms of the Jewish community, this had the effect of freeing these agents from the hold of the community potentates.

The weak position taken by a Fez sage in a decision in 1890 is typical of the new situation that had arisen. The case involved a group of merchants who had reached an agreement to pay jointly the extortions imposed upon them by Muslim potentates. Some of the partners to the agreement succeeded, however, in obtaining foreign citizenship and consular protection. Consequently, these merchants automatically became free of the impositions of local potentates. Thereupon they refused to honor their agreement with the other merchants, and the latter took the matter to court. The sage decided in favor of the plaintiffs, that in principle the agreement remained binding. However, he went on to advise them to settle out of court. Otherwise, the sage argued, the plaintiffs were prone to an accusation of "interfering in a matter that does not concern them" (Y. Ibn-Danan 7). This weak judgment reflects the new situation of many indigent Moroccan institutions, Jewish and probably also Muslim, at the end of traditional times. The institutions were hampered in their operation because of the novel element of foreign power that had moved onto the scene of Moroccan politics. This element lacked legitimization and therefore, in theory, did not change the authority relationships in society, but in practice much did change. In the Jewish community, some individuals now maintained particular ties with powerful foreigners, besides the numerous individuals who maintained such ties with Muslim potentates. All these ties were distinct from and sometimes contradicted the ties that bound people within Jewish society. In the chapter that follows we consider how these external factors impinged upon the character of Jewish self-rule in the communities.

4 SELF-RULE I:

INDIVIDUALS AND *NEGIDIM*

Jewish existence in precolonial Morocco was not founded on universal human rights, not even on specific civil rights. In theory, the status of the Jews was determined by general Muslim principles governing the status of the dhimmi minorities. In actuality, the position of Jews fluctuated widely over time and place, their livelihood and security depending upon the vicissitudes of their relationships with the local potentates. To the extent that the people of the communities were able to maintain their part of tacit agreements and understandings with the potentates, their situation remained secure. That part of the agreements entailed supplying goods and craftsmanship to the potentates, and in particular cash in the cities, where there was a money market.

The efficient organization of the potential of the mellah people to satisfy these material requests was a major political need of the communities, for on that the welfare of whole communities depended. The sonorous pronouncement of the Fez sages in this matter, in 1738, is eloquent:

> And the prime charity (*rosh ha'sedaqot*) in the world is the paying of taxes. For that establishes order (*ma'amedet ha'dat*) . . . so as to appease adversaries who oppress us always, . . . who [aim to] destroy the heritage of the Lord. And when we give them taxes and extortions we close the mouths of the evil ones. (Seifer ha'taqanot 88)

The acute realization of this need led to the maintenance of a system of internal self-rule, securing the procuration of funds to ward off "the evil ones." Besides the crucial matter of taxation for external political purposes, the communities were also active in internal affairs such as maintenance of law and order, religion, education, and welfare. The sources of the period evince many terms for social roles and institutions in these various areas of self-rule. In the present chapter we delineate the major public roles of Moroccan-Jewish society, following them in action.

The main concepts that figure are "individual" (*yahid*), "prince" (*nagid*, pl. *negidim*), "judge" (*dayan*), "sage" (*hakham*), "court-of-law" (*beit-din*), "seven elders" (*shive'at tuvei ha'ir*), "committee" (*ma'amad*), "administrator" (*parnas*). Of these concepts, the last three figure infrequently, less than they do in earlier sources of the sixteenth and seventeenth centuries. Often they appear in abstract general discussions. This indicates that institutions such as "the seven elders" figured in people's conceptions, but in reality they were not very vital.[1] In actuality, we find the incumbents of three roles most active in community self-government: "the individuals," "the nagid," and "the judge."

The individuals, adult males of such economic standing as to be taxpayers, are the source of ultimate authority in the community, and this authority is expressed when the individuals gather and enact regulations (*taqanot*). The system of community legislation, as operated by the individuals, was not highly formalized. There were no clear rules determining procedural matters, such as the composition of the gatherings, the quorum, and the voting requirements necessary for legislation. Also, the executive arm of the corporate community government was not highly developed. There was hardly any public officialdom for the day-to-day management of important community affairs such as taxation, education, and charity. Even the judicial system, the pride of Jewish self-government everywhere, functioned mostly without public officials. All these activities were maintained by the private initiative of people who offered their services to the public and received payment from clients for each transaction. This system governed the work of functionaries such as teachers, ritual slaughterers (*shohatim*), managers of ritual baths, and even judges. The latter however, as we shall see in detail in a later chapter, also had their independent economic base in the unique Moroccan private synagogue system. The nagid only is materially dependent upon the corporate community; we devote the latter part of this chapter to an elucidation of that role.

Concurrently with the lack of an elaborate and formalized public administration in the communities, we find much spontaneous involvement in public affairs on the part of people who lack any mandate to take action. A complex late eighteenth-century case (probably from Meknes) illustrates these conditions vividly. A man had evaded paying his taxes, and the community was helpless. Thereupon "one [of the community] supported by the ruler (*ehad meihem be'koah ha'serara*)" took hold of some of the tax-evader's property, sold it, and transferred the proceeds to the community as duly paid taxes. The evader then sued the community for the return of these funds. The court decreed that part was indeed due to him because the proceedings of the sale had exceeded the tax assessment. Now arose the question of the responsibility of the community, or, alternatively, of the individual who had confronted the evader, for the sum due to be returned. The court ruled:

> The individual took [the property from the evader] and gave it to the community. The latter did not take it [from the evader] . . . The community is [therefore] not liable (R. Berdugo 1891:244)

The judgment exonerated the corporate public body and laid full responsibility onto the violent "good Samaritan." This reflects conditions where the scope of corporate action is limited and where, on the other hand, the scope for individual action on behalf of the public is wide. The individual, therefore, bears unrelieved responsibility for his doings.

Occasionally, in the sources, we come across appointed officials who are public servants in the sense that they receive an overall salary for their services. However, here too, the system remains profoundly individualistic, far from any impersonal bureaucratic formality. An early nineteenth-century case conveys the atmosphere well. It concerns an unidentified, probably small, community, where a sage received a fixed salary in return for a wide range of services; that of ritual slaughterer, prayer leader, and teacher. The sage used to practice his slaughtering in a somewhat distant spot, away from the market, far from the Muslim slaughterers. One year, on the day before Passover, there was much pressure from clients, and they prevailed upon the harassed slaughterer to work in a more convenient spot, near the market. This aroused the ire of the Muslim slaughterers,[2] and they caused the community slaughterer to be fined. The problem that the Jewish court had to resolve was to determine who was to bear the expense caused by this mishap. The court ruled that the slaughterer was solely responsible and that no one need participate in paying the damages (Maimon Bergudo, Hoshen mishpat 246). The significance of this is that the community is not responsible for the acts of an official when he strays from the terms of his position, even though, in this case, the mitigating circumstances were obvious. In both the case of "the good Samaritan" and that of the harassed slaughterer, there emerges in these court decisions a conception of highly delimited public responsibility. Ambiguous acts are considered to be the acts of individuals, although the public benefited from them, and plausibly they might also have been considered as acts of the public.

This very narrow public element in communal appointments appears also in other elements of the political system of the communities, particularly in the legislation. This was invested primarily in gatherings of individuals, and we turn to examine the extent of the formalization of these conventions. A Sefrou regulation states that whatever is decided by fourteen named individuals is binding, and anyone who demurs will be punished by the nagid (Ovadia 16). From Tetuan we have the affirmation of a judge that "anything decided upon by four or five of the leaders (*rashim*) is binding" because, he explains apologetically, "in this place we do not have the system of 'seven elders'" (Khalfon: 49–50). The sages who adjudicated disputes surrounding local legislation would clearly have preferred the legislation to have been taken unanimously, or at least by a majority of the individuals (Mordekhay Berdugo 5; Elmaleh 29). But barring that, they allowed for another possibility to legitimize local legislation, namely, that the proposed ruling be publicly announced, and that it become binding if it does not arouse protest. Thus:

> The prevailing custom in all the cities of the Maghreb, when desiring to enact a regulation, is for the heads of the community and men of the committee, together with the sages of the city who are appointed over them, to come together . . . and write the regulation. They send it to all the synagogues in the city to read it [publicly] on the Sabbath, and the announcement constitutes acquiescence. If they did not protest they cannot reverse. (Ben-Walid: 96)

That this rule was the common practice is clear from the fact that it is recounted frequently in the sources, not only as an abstract regulation but also as an actuality (Ben-Walid: 94–96; R. M. Elbaz, Hoshen mishpat 128; Y. Ibn-Danan: 76b). The loosely defined conditions of this rule, however, left room for many misunderstandings and disputes over the legitimacy of specific acts of the community leaders. A case in point is a dispute that erupted in Tetuan in connection with the establishment of a new private synagogue, after a prohibition to do so had been enacted. The owner of the synagogue claimed that the prohibition was invalid because it had been signed only by the sages of the local court and not by the individuals of the community. Also, he argued, the regulation had not been announced in public. The judge rejected the plea of the synagogue owner, arguing that this particular regulation did not require publicity because it pertained only to sages whose doings involved them in synagogues. It did not pertain to ordinary people. Therefore, it sufficed that the town sages knew of the regulation. The judge expressed himself heatedly:

> Just think of it! A regulation that pertains only to the seven elders—do all the people, children and women have to know of it? And one that pertains to men only—does it have to be announced to the women? That is nonsense! (Monsoniego 12, see also 11, 13)

Thus public announcement was required only for regulations that concerned numerous people, such as those regarding taxation matters. Therefore, this judge concluded, the disputed synagogue had been founded illegally.

A Rabat dispute illuminates the practical difficulties of community legislation from another angle. The problem concerned a newly opened store that was situated near the ritual bath (*miqve*) used by women for their monthly purification, prior to reunion with their husbands. It was the popular belief, unfounded in rabbinic teaching, that a woman's first chance encounter, after emerging from purification, is of spiritual importance to the child likely to be conceived that night. It was deemed preferable that the woman's eyes should fall on a righteous Jew. Due to the proximity of the store to the miqve, however, the Muslim customers who patronized it were often the first people the women saw when coming from the ritual bath. Therefore, the women often felt obliged to return and immerse themselves again. Due to the primitive, and sometimes actually dangerous conditions of ritual bathing places, this was felt to be a great inconvenience. Therefore "some of the community" decreed the closure of the store. The owner took the matter to court and won his case. The court declared:

> This regulation does not pertain to a matter that is fundamental to religion (*seyag le'issur likhvod ha'torah*), therefore the minority is not obliged to obey the majority—and even when the regulation is buttressed by a threat of excommunication. (Elmaleh, vol. 2, 21, see also 4)

The sage evades examining the pertinent details of the legislative procedure. He dwells only on the content of the regulation and declares it invalid because, in his view, the public does not have a mandate to govern when motivated by what he considers a triviality. The judge evidently also considered it easier to resolve the case that way than by confronting the legislative procedure.

The highly informal legislative process was pervaded with vagueness, both on the level of substance and the level of procedure. This led to the practice of enacting regulations in gatherings of numerous individuals (sometimes numbering dozens) and in the presence of sages. Such enactments were weighty, while those produced by a small number of community leaders, particularly when not coordinated with the sages, were of little consequence. The informality of the process lent particular weight to the adjudicative role that the sages filled, as disputes stemming from dubious legislation were brought to the attention of the courts.

Crucially, however, the autonomy of the sages in their judicial roles was not unhampered. The sages were well aware that there were high-handed individuals in the communities over whom they were powerless. A Sefrou sage writes about these conditions in general:

> If at any time a high-handed individual or individuals (*adam ya-hid o rabim*) arise, [he should be] taken to the Torah court . . . if possible. And if that is not possible one should wait until the hand of that violator will fall. (Ovadia 17a)

Similarly, in an earlier chapter we saw Ibn-Sur vacillate as a result of powerful ligitants involving their Muslim patrons. More generally, Ibn-Sur writes with extraordinary candor:

> And who can call them to law, and who is the judge who can adjudicate them and convict them? It is clear that even if they will stand in judgment the judge must sometimes ignore things, otherwise he will suffer damage . . . And I have experienced such situations myself. (Ibn-Sur, vol. 2, 173)

From Salé we learn of a man who had been convicted of homosexuality and forbidden by the Jewish court from participating in synagogue services (a form of partial excommunication). Thereupon the offender was invited by a powerful individual who owned a synagogue to worship there. The man received public honors in that synagogue and, with these, respectability (A. Anqawe 37).

In another incident a man wedded a woman in the presence of a quorum of ten men, but without a sage. There was "only a junior sage (*talmid hakham*)[3] who was a prayer leader and teacher; but the regulations say that there must be a sage." The case involved deciding upon the marital status of the couple. The judge ruled that the preferred solution to the complex problem of marital status that had developed was for the couple to get divorced and then remarry properly. He concludes, "And that is the proper way if he is a law-abiding person (*gavra de'saita le'dina*)" (Ibn-Sur 206). The sage was thus clearly aware of the limits of his power, differentiating among the people of the community between those who are law-abiding and others who are not and beyond the arm of the law (see also R. Berdugo 1942, vol. 2:61). The notion that people do not always stand equal before the law is rooted in the general conditions of Moroccan politics and society (that we saw in Chapter 2). Moreover, it does not seem to have always been conceived by the mellah people as a foreign intrusion into Jewish self-government. Here is the comment of a Rabat sage on the doings of the elders of a community vis-à-vis an individual:

> It is being said that he is one of the individuals of the community and bears the yoke with all, the yoke of taxes, impositions, hosting of sojourners, and so forth. It is [therefore] inappropriate to be harsh with him . . . to exclude him, even though he did act improperly. (Elmaleh, vol. 2: 6b)

A nineteenth-century sage makes a general observation that reflects the altogether weak rule of the law:

> There are daily occurences (*ma'asim bekhol yom*) where [people] transgress regulations that are backed by [threat of] excommunication . . . and one does not apply the law . . . One does not even have a sage (*le'ha'amid sheliah sibbur*) declare the [threat of] excommunication to be void. (A. Anqawe 6)

The breaches in communal authority were linked to the situation that we have encountered, of powerful individuals who were backed by potentates beyond the Jewish community. Besides that, however, there were elements inherent in the structure of the rabbinical role that stymied the formalization of communal authority. The religious leaders of the communities, including the judges, were predominantly indigenous members of the communities in which they functioned. The sages were members of local families, and local affairs that sometimes led to animosity between families doubtlessly also embroiled those family members who were sages. The membership of the sages in local families sometimes encumbered them in filling judicial roles because members of rival families might have reservations about the impartiality of the judge, and the judge himself might wish to avoid such situations (Ibn-Sur 6). The condition one Sefrou sage made upon being appointed judge is typical: he stipulated that all local people agree to his adjudication, even when the opposing party was related to him (Ovadia 28; see also 92, 167).

In practice, however, matters were different. We learn of cases that could not be heard locally because of kin ties between one of the parties and the judge, and the latter's fears that he might arouse hostility against himself (Ovadia 92). Such cases must have been frequent, because ties of kin within the communities were tightknit, as we shall see in a later chapter. Taking a lawsuit to another community was an involved matter, and there was no way to coerce a dissenting party to travel there. Further, even when the parties agreed, travel itself was no light matter. Finally, as discussed in Chapter 2, sometimes a party was inhibited from traveling to a certain locality because of the complexities of relationships that prevailed between his Muslim patron and other potentates. This sometimes caused judgment to be given in the presence of one party only; and we may presume that this did not ease the administration of justice.

The role of nagid is another major political role in the communities, besides that of the individuals who formulated regulations and that of the sages who certified their legality and adjudicated disputes. The role of the nagid comprises two functions: adjudication according to the lay system of local customary law, and representation of the community vis-à-vis the Muslim authorities. Since the second function is intimately linked with monetary expenses, the nagid also administered communal taxation.

First, the adjudicative role. The historical sources that serve us were predominantly written by sages, and largely reflect conditions as seen from the rabbinical perspective. In the sphere of legal matters it is natural that these sources highlight the judicial doings of the sages, who practiced the divine law of the Torah—the pride and virtual raison d'être of the stratum of sages. However, many (perhaps most) communities in Morocco and other Jewish societies maintained a parallel system of lay law. Since this was not run by the learned, it left comparatively few literary traces. Those indications that have been preserved in the rabbinical responsa are therefore particularly important. From the testimony of two eighteenth-century Fez and Meknes sages, we learn the following principle:

> Concerning taxes: It is accepted throughout the diaspora that anyone who owes the community is locked in jail, and is not brought to judgment before the court-of-law (*beit din*). The town elders judge him according to their custom (Elkhreif 11; see also Yoseif Berdugo I, 1922–1943, vol. 3: 33b; M. Toledano: 57b).[4]

Besides this general statement, we have on hand a number of cases where we hear of the lay system in action. In 1728 a Fez home was violently broken into. The owner, suspecting a certain member of the community of having hired the felons, complained to the nagid, and the latter had the suspect jailed.[5] Eventually the complicated case came to court before the sages, and the homeowner was asked why he had not complained to the court. His reply was, "It is common practice to report such matters only to the nagid." Eventually the sages called upon the nagid to release the suspect, and he ignored them (Ibn-Sur 116). The case clearly reflects an established practice of adjudication in certain matters by the nagid. Another such case has come to us that involved a man and a woman who had sexual relations without being married. The source reports, that "the nagid and the individuals of the community fined [the man] ten metkalim for the ruler (*serara*) and the poor"[6] (Ya'aqov Berdugo, Even ha'ezer 83). Given the fact that the lay judges were not given to write about their rulings,[7] and that these few cases figure only incidentally in the writings of the sages, they are probably representative of many others.

The small number of cases of lay adjudication that we have on hand does not permit us to trace a clear delimitation between the scope of lay justice as administered by the nagid and that of halakhic justice as adjudicated by the sages. But the material does provide some indications. It appears that the nagid governed matters that were considered grave by society, such as illicit sex and personal violence. On the other hand, the great majority of the cases that came before the sages concerned the complexities of property ownership and of marital status. The sages thus expended their craft primarily on the complications that are inherent in the daily activities of law-abiding people, not on the doings of lawbreakers. For the latter, heavy fines and corporal punishment were considered appropriate. But such punishment could be administered only with the active cooperation of Muslim potentates beyond the community, who wielded the implements of force. Hence the nagid and his associates, themselves important clients of powerful patrons, were in a position to punish lawbreakers. But the sages, as we shall see in a later chapter, were not usually in a position to enable them to mobilize external potentates. The judicial power of the lay leaders thus dovetailed that of the sages, and the one supported the other.

Besides the fact that lay justice was based on age-old custom, the sages sometimes explicitly affirmed the right of the nagid to adjudicate. In a document affirming the appointment of a Sefrou nagid, the sages declare his prerogative "to incarcerate, fine and punish, both corporally and monetarily . . . anyone who strays from the path of goodness and uprightness" (S. Y. Abitbul 64). Indeed, the power inherent in the role of the nagid vis-à-vis his Muslim patron often permitted him to act as the executive arm of rabbinical justice. Occasionally, therefore, we encounter legislation sanctioned by the sages that established fixed fines and determined that the nagid execute the punishment (Ovadia 1985, 48).

The second function of the nagid, the maintenance of relationships between the community and Muslim potentates, required him to have ready access to large sums of money. Fundamentally this need stemmed from the situation of the dhimmi among Muslims, in which the imposition of discriminative taxation was not a matter of mere rapacity but of theological import.[8] Taxation of that nature, however, was only a minor financial burden in our period. The high-handed greed of Muslim potentates that erupted erratically, as attested by the chronicles, was fueled by ordinary human passions, and those were the major concerns of the nagid.

He faced not only actual governors (the monarch and his local representative, or independent tribal leaders) but also innumerable courtiers and gatekeepers—actual and figurative—who surrounded the governors. All those expected, and often demanded, to be given their portions. From the perspective of the potentates, the nagid was primarily an individual, albeit powerful, Jew, not an official of the community. They were familiar with the nagid in his private capacity as a man of commerce, and to some of them he probably stood in a patron-client relationship. At the same time, the Muslim potentates were not much involved or interested in the internal details of Jewish community politics. The result was that, when the potentates addressed demands to the community, they in fact addressed them to the nagid in person. And the feeling of the people about these potentates was that "their wrath is constant, and they hurt everyone who acts for the public" (Ovadia 1985, 33).

Because of this situation, we encounter the phenomenon of negidim who insist on being accompanied by other men of the community when appearing before the potentates. The apprehension of negidim to act solitarily is such, that, upon appointment, they sometimes specify the names of the individuals who are to stand by their side at such encounters (Ovadia 1985, 52; S. Y. Abitbul 64). Clearly, the aim of the nagid is that the demands of the potentates be shared with others and not shouldered by him alone. Indeed, the chronicles and other sources are replete with accounts of community representatives who suffered at the hands of potentates, both in their property and in their person. People naturally tried to avoid hazardous encounters with the potentates.

The lack of clear demarcation between the private and public roles that the nagid filled aroused practical difficulties in the financing of his public activities. A recurrent problem in financial disputes involving the nagid and the members of his community was the question of remuneration for expenses that the nagid claimed to have incurred in the course of filling his public duties. The sages had recurrently to decide whether a certain payment by the nagid to a potentate was for the benefit of the public or for his own benefit. One such case involved a nagid who had exerted himself to release a man imprisoned by Muslims. In the course of doing so the nagid had an encounter with a Muslim enemy of his, and the latter accused him of having cursed the Islamic faith. The accusation, which involved danger to the nagid's life, necessitated his giving bribes in order to be released. But the community rejected the nagid's claim for reimbursement, arguing in court that "his own [bad] luck" had caused the mishap (A. Elbaz 14). The public's understanding of the nature of the community role was thus narrowly delimited (as we also saw earlier in the cases of the hotheaded Good Samaritan and of the harassed slaughterer). In this case, however, the court supported the nagid. The sage mustered legal arguments in favor of the claimant, but significantly he concluded with a practical, extralegal consideration. The sage ruled that the community was obliged to come to a settlement with the nagid. For, otherwise, no one would in the future agree to fill the role of nagid, and for lack of effective external representation "any [Muslim potentate] who felt like taking would just come and take."

The structure of the role of the nagid commonly led to situations where community expenses were paid by him out of his personal resources. Theoretically the community was obliged to reimburse these expenses, and clauses to that effect commonly recur in the appointment agreements of negidim. The implementation of the principle was, however, as we saw, fraught with difficulty. There was a further recurring problem. Was the person who claimed reimbursement in the role of nagid entitled to actually entail public expenses? Or was he no public official at all? The problem arose in situations where the nagid was a powerful person who had his ties with Muslim potentates, and the latter appointed him to the position of nagid. This was particularly the case in eighteenth-century Meknes, when it served as the preferred 'Alawi capital. When the Muslim rulers initiated dealings with the community concerning monetary requests, in particular, they would do so through the offices of their appointee. In such cases, the sages ruled that the appointment was binding upon the community (Ibn-Sur 115; H. Toledano 94), and the nagid was entitled to reimbursement. However, where the community had protested against an appointment but had been high-handedly overruled by the Muslim potentate and his Jewish client, the sage ruled that the community was not liable for the nagid's expenses. These rulings express the partial autonomy of the communities in their appointments, and the sometimes considerable interference of the authorities in internal Jewish politics.

The standing of any particular nagid in the community is determined less by the formal parameters of the role of nagid than by idiosyncratic factors pertaining to his own relationships with Muslim potentates and to his individual personality. While becoming nagid is a public appointment—often defined by the clauses of a formal document—he is not clearly subject to the individuals whose authority it is to appoint him. Ibn-Sur offers a general observation:

> It is well-known that all appointed officials in our times (*kol memunei ha'zeman*) cannot escape the following: lowering the tax-assessment of one [person] and raising that of another [person], and thus collecting from many people more than is due. (Ibn-Sur, vol. 2, 185)

He concludes, severely, that nagidim should be considered to be "tax-masters . . . and not . . . managers [of charities]" (*din mokheis . . . ve'lo . . . din gabai*).[9] This harsh evaluation reflects negidim who act as agents of despots and not as representatives of their communities.[10]

We have on hand, however, an equally general observation signed by a court of three Fez sages one century later, which is diametrically opposite that of Ibn-Sur. The sages write,

> Our eyes see all the negidim who serve the public (*ha'omedim al ha'sibbur*)—not one of them enters the position whole and leaves it whole. They are more likely to suffer damage than not to suffer. (A. Elbaz 14; see also Ovadia 99)

This testimony presumably refers to situations where negidim are unable to fill the excessive demands of the pertinent potentates, and consequently they suffer. Both Ibn-Sur and the later sages are veteran judges, and their testimonies are reliable. The discrepancy, therefore, calls for attention.

Ibn-Sur's observation is based on his experience in Fez and Meknes in the first half of the eighteenth century, the later sages on their experience one century later. Clearly, one cannot harmonize these observations by assuming that all the nineteenth-century officials were upright and those of the eighteenth-century all villains. It is more probable that the despotic rulers of the eighteenth-century royal cities permitted less leeway to the nagid than did the weaker rulers of a century later. Therefore, the nineteenth-century negidim did not need to press their coreligionists as hard as did their predecessors.[11] The activities of the negidim are linked closely with those of the Muslim rulers and reflect the overall policies, and particularly the financial needs, of the latter. Abrupt changes of political fortune, policy, and whims of the rulers led to erratic shifts in the fortunes of their courtiers (see Hirschberg 1981: 289–291, for references to the vicissicitudes that befell some of the Jewish courtiers). The differences in fulfilling the public role of nagid should be seen, then, as depending primarily on the vagaries of external politics and of individual personalities, and on the particular relationships that prevailed between a given nagid and the Muslim authorities. The functioning of the role of nagid as determined by the formal rules of the communities is secondary.

The preferred mode of appointment to the position of nagid was by election of the general assembly of the individuals, as the late eighteenth-century Sefrou sage, Rabbi Sha'ul Yeshu'a Abitbul, writes:

> The common custom in all the places is, that the individuals of the city send for the person who seems to be outstanding (*she'nir'a be'alil*), and is desirable for activity, and install him . . . and that constitutes his appointment.

The apparently independent authority of the individuals expressed in this general statement is illusory. In actual cases of appointment, the local sages figure actively, at the side of the laymen (Ovadia 93, 187). Further, there are indications that the sages saw themselves as an independent source of authority for such appointments, parallel to that of the laymen. Thus, in one letter of appointment, after the signature of the individuals, the sages prefaced their own signatures with the following statement:

> And after the community agreed upon him and appointed him we also, the undersigned court-of-law, have agreed . . . And we have set him up as nagid over the public just as the community has set him up . . . We have given full permission and authority to the forementioned R. Elazar to be appointed as nagid over them.[12] (S. Y. Abitbul 64)

After resolution of the problems concerning the allocation of responsibility for the expenses incurred by the nagid, there remained the issue of actual repayment. This was rooted in the state of institutionalization of the community financial organs. Monetary development in Sherifian Morocco stood at a low level; specifically, there were no organizations that specialized in the advancement of credit. The owners of capital usually invested in commercial doings, and there was no substantially developed market for liquid capital. In the Jewish communities, the community treasury did not usually have substantial sums of money available when needed. The communities did own some landed property,[13] particularly stores, residences (Ovadia 1975–1985, vol. 4, 35), and occasionally synagogues (as we shall see in Chap. 7), that had accrued to the community as pious endowments (*heqdeish*). But this property does not seem to have been quantitatively very significant. Moreover, even when such community property was considerable, it did not afford much actual income, since the stores and apartments were not rented on the free market but were placed at the disposal of the deserving poor and of the sages. Hence, no substantial income flowed from them to the community treasury.

Another source of community income was the imposition of indirect taxes by the community on various commercial transactions and on the purchase of consumer goods. In particular, there was the imposition of a tax on the purchase of kosher meat. But the sources do not give rise to the impression that these taxes were very regularly instituted, nor that they were of major monetary substance (see Chap. 5 for the taxation system). Moneys that accrued from indirect taxes mostly served the needs of the poor and were not used for external impositions. The summary conclusion, then, is that the communities had no regular readily available funds for the needs of the nagid.

The common practice for a nagid seeking reimbursement was to turn to individuals in the community. The procedure was direct and personal and did not involve a formal community treasury. A Sefrou agreement between a nagid and his community indicates that the nagid had the privilege of demanding reimbursement from anyone out of nineteen individuals who signed the agreement. The document goes on to specify that the latter may then turn "to the public in general" (*kelalut ha'sibbur*), in order to be reimbursed (Ovadia 422). A similar arrangement emerges from a Tetuan source. An individual owed a sum of money to the community, and the latter owed money to the nagid. The sage ruled that the nagid be reimbursed directly by the individual (Ben-Malka 136). In a Meknes case in which "all the community owed money to an individual," the sage ruled that he could sue anyone of the community (Yoseif Berdugo I, 1922–1943, vol. 2: 5). Evidently, in all these communities, both the large Tetuan and Meknes and the small Sefrou communities, there was no orderly communal treasury.

The implication of these arrangements for the reimbursement of public expenses was that negidim did not usually pay taxes, for tax exemption was a way to obtain reimbursement (Ovadia 1975–1985, vol. 4, 42). Further, it is reasonable to hypothesize that a nagid who had no legal monetary claims on the community was a high-handed potentate, who engaged in inordinate extortions of taxes and bribes for himself and for his Muslim patron. In a Sefrou case we even hear of the legalized exemption of negidim from taxation, not just de facto exemption. A certain individual was named for the position of nagid, and the nomination included various considerations in support of the proposal. One of them was that the said person was already president of the charitable burial society (*hevrat gemilut hesed*), and as such he was exempt from taxation. Those in favor of his candidacy thus found a virtue in the fact that appointment to the position of nagid would save the community an additional tax exemption (Ovadia 187).

The element of personalization and informality is evident also in a recurring clause in letters appointing negidim. This clause concerns the details of verifying the claims of negidim and stipulates that the nagid need not make his claim under oath, as would be the normal judicial procedure. He need no more than declare his expenses, and his statement would be accepted by the individuals (Ovadia 24; 1975–1985, vol. 4, 15). But such a clause does not assure the nagid that, in fact, the individuals will have funds at hand that they are both able and willing to part with when requested. This is the background to the case of a Sefrou nagid whom the community reimbursed by giving him a store that was owned by the community (Ovadia 422). Thereby, the altogether weak politico-economic base of the community was weakened yet further.

We are now in a position to summarize the salient sociological characteristic of the role of nagid. Despite its importance in community self-government, the role was not highly formalized; it was filled in variegated ways at different times and places. This characteristic of the role of nagid leads us to appreciate the importance in community politics of the sage, who acts as judge. In contrast to the nagid, the sage filled a much more formalized, differentiated role. The sages of precolonial Morocco operated on the base of a venerable tradition, going back to antiquity, that emphasized the moral and professional integrity of the judicial role. This tradition was deeply entrenched, one of the fundamentals of halakha in all Jewish societies. Consequently, the judicial system of the sages operated in a virtually predetermined groove that could be anticipated. While the role of nagid was subject to fluctuations, that stemmed from the conditions that we have seen, the leadership that the sages provided was a major anchor of stability in the communities. This applied to both the judicial and the other roles (such as in religious, educational, and welfare matters) that the sages filled. However, the sages, too, were part of mellah society, and their doings featured characteristics that dovetailed with other elements of Sherifian times.

In the next chapter we focus on a specific problem of mellah self-rule, the system of taxation which involved both the negidim and the sages. And in Chapter 6 we turn to a detailed examination of the doings of the sages in their communities.

5 SELF RULE II:
THE TAXATION
AND CHARITY SYSTEM

We have seen the frailty of some of the seams of mellah self-rule, in the roles of individuals and of *negidim*. This is rooted both in exigencies that are external to the Jewish communities and in the nature of the internal political system of the communities. In the present chapter we focus on one crucially important communal activity, the levying of taxes.

The welfare of the people of the mellah depended, in the last resort, upon their ability to pay for their physical security. This necessitated the maintenance of an effective system of taxation. The system was structured to draw funds both for the external political needs of the community and for internal needs that were primarily of a welfare and cultural nature. The expenses for internal community needs were considered as charities, religiously mandated. Moneys for the payment of external communal taxes, bribes, and extortions were collected by a system of direct taxation. The predominant practice of the communities was to appoint a small number of assessors who determined the amount each individual was obliged to pay. These assessments were based on the estimated amount of the property and volume of business of the individuals. On the other hand, moneys necessary for internal community needs of a welfare and religious nature were obtained by indirect taxation. Sometimes these funds were obtained as voluntary donations which, however, were bolstered by more or less subtle social pressure, in which the self-respect of individuals was manipulated.

The head tax mentioned in the previous chapter was of great political and symbolic import for the standing of the communities. Materially, however, it was of minor importance, relative to the frequent indeterminate and irregular impositions of the potentates. Acquiescing to these secular impositions, that were devoid of symbolic trappings, was essential for the physical protection of the communities of unarmed minority merchants and craftsmen exposed to armed insurgents of the majority population. Whenever the need arose for the payment of bribes and protection money to Muslim potentates, the community set in motion the aforementioned procedure for the collection of direct taxes. There was also a system whereby the individuals declared by oath, before their peers, the amount that they were in a position to pay. That system was an obvious invitation to abuse, as wealthy people were likely to underassess themselves. The outcome of that system was that the masses of people of middle and low income were burdened relatively more than the wealthy.

The sages were particularly apprehensive that poor people burdened with heavy taxation might defect and convert to Islam, if their taxation burden was not eased (Ibn-Sur 202). And we saw earlier that defections did occur at times of famine and other crises. The sages were concerned with an additional problem: the apprehension that husbands and fathers in dire straits might desert their families, leaving their wives in a legal state of *aguna*.[1] Further, an inequitable taxation system might lead people to have increased recourse to the assistance of Muslim potentates (Ovadia 136). Consequently, the sages preferred an assessment procedure that did not permit the wealthy to shirk so easily the brunt of the burden of taxation, namely, the aforementioned assessment by committee (Ibn-Sur 211).

Since our available sources are rabbinic, they contain an inbuilt bias to reflect the conditions that obtained wherever the opinion of sages was weighty. It is, therefore, plausible that in small localities, where there were no authoritative sages, the taxation assessments were sometimes made according to the inequitable preference of wealthy community laymen, namely, by self-assessment. In the large communities, aside from the activities of sages, there was another pertinent factor, namely, population size, that favored assessment by committee. Where the population of the community amounted to dozens, perhaps hundreds of taxpayers, there naturally emerged a sociological process of formalization. In terms of taxation this implied assessment by appointed community officers. We have a report that in the first years of the eighteenth century the Fez procedure was markedly impersonal and bureaucratized. There were three teams of three assessors each to scan the large community, and each team was composed of one representative of the merchants, one of the craftsmen, and a sage who acted as chairman (Ibn-Sur 211; for the Sefrou procedure see Ovadia 233, 473).

The Fez procedure is attuned to the structure of a community that is not only large but differentiated, in the sense that it has a powerful stratum of craftsmen, besides the merchants, as we saw in Chapter 3. Other communities, as we saw there, did not have such a social balance to their dominant stratum of merchants. Consequently, the silence of the sources of the other communities, as to the existence of social differentiation in their assessment committees, might reasonably be interpreted as reflecting the actual lack of such differentiation. The Fez report represents the ultimate in the formalization of tax assessment procedures in precolonial Moroccan Jewry.

In contrast to the particular Fez system, there was a universal custom in Moroccan Jewry—including Fez—that reflects the powerful hold of the personal, informal element in public life. It was accepted that if, upon conclusion of the tax assessment, the highest assessment slot was filled by only one individual, that person was downgraded and taxed in a lower slot, together with the next highest assessed individual. The overt rationale for this practice was that an individual who filled a taxation slot by himself was thereby dangerously exposed to covetous, predatory potentates (Ibn-Sur 249). The custom aimed to protect the outstanding wealthy person from such exposure. While in the context of the conditions of the times, the rationale was realistically plausible, the custom also blatantly favored the powerful individual at the expense of everyone else in the community.

Besides the direct taxation of individuals, we encounter surcharge taxation imposed on specific categories of individuals in connection with their source of income or domestic consumption. Thus, we hear of merchants being taxed on the base of the value of the merchandise they brought through the city gates (Schroeter n.d.; Ibn-Sur 209; Ovadia 1975–1985, vol 3: 55). Sometimes, as in Mogador, the tax was collected by Muslim collectors posted at the city gates. But where the Muslim authorities lacked a suitable officialdom, the collection of these surcharges was entrusted to a Jewish client of the potentate, or to the community. The latter might then farm out collection of the surcharge tax to one of the individuals of the community. Thus, sociologically, the collection of taxes from a specific category of individuals was not different from general tax collection, governed by the nagid, that we encountered in the previous chapter. We hear of a community that tried its hand at such surcharge taxation of particular categories of people to cover its own needs (Elmaleh, vol. 2, 4). It is clear, however, from the account of the case, that this taxation practice of the community was illicit in the eyes of the Muslim authorities.[2] Such

taxation by the community, in a fashion parallel to that of the authorities, probably aroused the rapacity of the potentates. It is also possible
that it caused affront to Muslim sensitivities as to the low political
profile that is appropriate to the dhimmi. Be that as it may, the communities were very circumspect in imposing taxation for their internal
needs. To those we turn now.

The most pressing requirement of the communities for funds, in the
area of internal affairs, was for the poor. Poverty was rampant, due to
the basic structure of the Moroccan Jewish economy, which did not
avail itself of the more lucrative niches of the general economy to meet
the needs of most of the mellah people. Also, the vagaries of pesti-
lences and wars caused havoc, leaving many people destitute, and
many orphans and widows. The communities were also beset with
wandering beggars, "guests" (orhim) as they are delicately called in the
sources. These beggars came from as far away as Eretz Israel, and even
Poland occasionally. The distant travelers were often dignified sages
who were emissaries from the communities of the Holy Land, and they
filled an important role in the religious life of many Diaspora communities. But economically, they, and others who had nothing to contribute to their hosts, were a burden. People were required to offer
home hospitality to uninvited guests for extended periods of time,
during which they collected donations from the community. Hospitality in the Moroccan context implied hosting on a much grander scale
than people would normally treat themselves, and the dignified guest
sages also had to be offered personal accompaniment in their begging
tours among the local people (Seifer ha'taqanot 155).

There were several ways of collecting funds for the needy. One was
for wealthy people to distribute money generously at irregular times,
whenever they celebrated a rite of passage in their families, or whenever they renovated their homes or initiated a major business venture. These donations were sometimes institutionalized to the extent
of amounting to a quarter or a third of the total expense (H. Toledano
105; Ovadia 17b). Another way of collecting funds for the needy was
by the imposition of an indirect tax on the purchase of ritually slaugh-
tered meat. In connection with these levies for the poor we hear of the
role of "supervisor of charity" (gabay sedaqa), or "treasurer of the poor"
(gizbar 'aniyim); also of "the charity fund" (qupat ha'sedaqa). These voluntary community officials were entrusted with the management of
landed property that generous individuals sometimes gave to the community, as endowment for the poor. Such property also sometimes

came to the community according to the rule, that heirless property went to the public (Ovadia 1975–1985, vol. 3: 54), and when such property was rented remuneratively, the proceeds were earmarked for the needy (R. M. Elbaz, Hoshen mishpat 72).

Such property, however, was often made available for the personal use of the needy, and therefore no income accrued from it (Ovadia 130). Further, we saw in the previous chapter that a nagid might recover expenses by appropriating to himself landed property of the community. The transfer of community property, presumably earmarked for the needy to a particular individual, dovetails such a practice. We hear of a case in Sefrou in the late nineteenth century, in connection with a pious individual who used to devote himself to the needs of the poor. The man had decided, as a culmination of his piety, to emigrate to the Holy Land to live out his years there. The community heads exerted themselves to convince him to remain in Sefrou so that the community could continue to benefit from his public services. They finally prevailed upon him by giving him "some rooms" that the community owned and used to rent out. In their account the community heads explained, "We considered that his staying here would be of greater benefit to the poor than the income [accruing] from these rooms" (Ovadia 125). Thus, while there was some formalization of welfare institutions in the mellah, this was precarious.

The preference one encounters in Moroccan culture, for individualization, operated against any incipient impersonal formality in the communities. One hears little in the sources of impersonal funds and organizations in the area of succor for the needy. To the extent that such funds did exist, we may assume that they were not of prime material importance, as against personalized and direct charity, which was more substantial. We have accounts on hand of two attempts at formalization and impersonalization of charity collection procedures, which depict the sociocultural forces that opposed formalization. In late nineteenth-century Meknes, a local sage sought to improve order in his synagogue by discouraging the local beggars from soliciting during services. He had charity boxes installed into which people were to place their donations anonymously, and once a month a synagogue official was to distribute the proceeds to the poor. The sage writes that various synagogue communities followed his example for about five years. Thereafter, however, they all gradually reverted to the traditional system (H. Meshash: 218).

From Fez (in 1848) we have an account of an attempt to lend permanence to the system of support for an Eretz Yisrael emissary:

> The sages and heads of our city, may the Lord guard them, decreed to establish a fund for the Maghrebi sages [of Jerusalem], besides the contribution made for them (*ha'nedava she'asu lahem*). The forementioned emissary exerted himself, and commissioned craftsmen to make small lead boxes, and distributed them to homes, so that everyone give a coin every week . . . then every month the managers (*gabaim*) will come to collect . . . and send [the money] to the Maghrebi sages. (Ovadia 1979, vol. 2: 318)

The impersonal innovation that the foreign emissary tried to introduce is clear. The context is the fact that after an Eretz Yisrael emissary departed the community, there rarely remained a permanent administration or local appointees to maintain ongoing activities for his cause, although contact with Eretz Yisrael emissaries was cherished.[3] This is in contrast to the situation in many communities in other parts of the Diaspora that did maintain such an administration. In the Fez attempt the local sages tried to assist the emissary—but whether people actually contributed according to the new system we are not informed. The innovation is so foreign to the way of life of Morocco that one may reasonably assume that it failed.

The communities also raised money in the course of religious activities. These funds were conceived in the context of *misva* (pl. *misvot*), a pious deed. Thus, the sages maintained themselves and the synagogues by auctioning various parts of the religious services, and thereby permitting the worshippers to be prominent in synagogue. This auctioning was termed "selling of misvot," and the purchasing was "buying misvot." The auctioning operated in the context of communities of worshippers and was powerfully molded by the informal social control of groups. Such also was the case of publicly announced voluntary donations in synagogue, which were termed gifts "in honor of the Torah" (*likhvod ha'torah*), in fact, gifts for the sage who personified the Holy Law.[4] Thus, as we move from moneys given for external public needs onto moneys given for internal individual needs, the levies are embedded ever more deeply in other social activities. Only bribes and extortions paid to Muslim potentates are raised from the public by an overt, direct, and specialized taxation system.

The difference between the two types of levies is salient in the many discussions in the sources about tax evasion and exemptions. The sources contain many cases concerning individuals who sought to relieve themselves of the burden of direct taxation. One type of such cases involves individuals who claim exemption on the basis of being sages. The principle of the tax exemption of sages is widely accepted in Jewish societies at all times. Litigation in this matter is mainly concerned with establishing the definition of the preferred category, and whether it applies to a given individual. It is remarkable that such cases are rare when the taxes in question are indirect; there seems to have been widespread acquiescence to pay those. Moreover, while there is some evidence of evasion of payment of surcharge taxes, instituted by the community on business dealings, there is virtually no evidence of people avoiding to host itinerant beggars and be generous to them. Also, there is no trace of evidence of people neglecting to make offerings "in honor of the Torah" to sages or to default on their promises. It is significant that the sages who jealously guarded their privilege of immunity from direct taxation accepted the obligation to pay the indirect surcharge tax on butchered meat (Ibn-Sur 213, 258). And they participated as a matter of course in all the levies that were conceived as misva, pious charities.

Besides the immunity of sages from direct taxation, which is based on considerations of religion, there were other categories of immunity based on welfare considerations. Thus, people defined as poor by the tax-assessment committees were not liable. Also, men aged sixty to seventy were freed from paying, if sickly, even though they were affluent; and above the age of seventy, they were freed even if vigorous and affluent (Ben-Malka 55; R. M. Elbaz, Hoshen mishpat 13). Besides these general principles governing immunity from taxation, there are deliberations in the sources about particular individuals who claimed exemption without being in the above categories. Thus, we hear of a person who devoted himself to hosting guests who was granted tax exemption (Ovadia 56). The implication of this is that an individual who devotes himself to the public good is entitled to material remuneration. But the community, due to its limited and weakly developed institutions, had no organ to extend such a benefit. Specifically, in the case of the care of travelers, there was no special guest house or fund out of which remuneration might have been drawn for the worthy individual. Therefore, the only option forthcoming for the community was to be lenient in its demands for direct taxes, its main and crucial source of material income. This practice dovetails with the remuneration procedure of negidim who brought the community taxes to the potentates (Chap. 4) and thereafter exempted themselves from taxation. All these practices reflect the limited formality and minimal bureaucratization of the community institutions in mellah society.

6   SELF-RULE III: THE SAGES

Since the communities viewed themselves as "holy communities" (*qehillot qodesh*), the lay individuals who legislated community matters required the support of Torah sages. Barring such support, the doings of community leaders were prone to be challenged as illegitimate. The more religious the support, in terms of the numbers and prestige of the sages who undersigned a particular act of lay legislation, the more authoritative it became. The sages thus filled important roles, beyond their particular expertise as adjudicators and moral leaders.

The broad category of "sages" included judges, ritual slaughterers, scribes of religious artifacts and documents, prayer leaders, and teachers.[1] The modern clerical role of spiritual guide, or pastor, did not exist separately from the aforementioned. Many people were also called "sages" who spent a good part of their working day studying Torah, and who restricted substantially the time they devoted to making a living. These people either studied at home by themselves, or in the synagogue with other scholars, and in that case they were referred to as "sages of the academy" (*hakhmey ha'yeshiva*) or "the association of enclosure (*hevrat ha'hesger*) (Ovadia 1979, vol. 2: 367; Ovadia 312, 629; Sefer ha'taqanot 155). The members of these circles were sometimes supported with regular stipends from wealthy individuals, who thereby attained a share in the religious merit of studying the holy law (Ovadia 75; A. Anqawe, Yoreh dei'a 36).[2]

A major source of support for the sages was their exemption from communal taxation on the income they gained from part-time commerce and handicrafts. At least in principle, such exemption was universal throughout traditional Jewry. In actuality, tax exemption of sages was a recurring bone of contention. Individual sages were naturally sensitive to any infringement of what they considered to be their rights, and the courts always supported them. In Morocco during our period, we encounter sages threatening to withhold their services from the public if their tax privileges were infringed upon. Sages also threatened to depart from their synagogues and to gather together in one synagogue, thus disrupting religious services (Ovadia 681).[3]

The ranking sages, who filled judicial roles, were appointed formally in one of several ways, of which the preferred one was appointment by a superior sage. This emerges vividly in a late eighteenth-century Sefrou rivalry case involving two judges who both had appointments in that small community. One of the protagonists, Rabbi Shlomo Abitbul, circulated an epistle of complaint in which he proudly described himself as having been appointed "by the word of the Fez sages" (al pi hakhmei Fas). About his rival, he writes disdainfully, "As to that judge—[the individuals] set him up by their own word" (ve'ze ha'dayan he'emiduhu al pi asmam).[4] The writer, and presumably the people whom by this argument he sought to sway in his favor, considered the democratic appointment of his rival by the community to be inferior to the kind of appointment that he had. Nevertheless, appointment by the individuals was common also. We have on hand acts of agreement of individuals that stipulate they will submit to the appointee's adjudication and not seek justice at the court of any other judge, even when there are kin ties between the judge and one of the disputants. There were also cases where the local individuals were not independent in appointments and subjected themselves to the involvement of powerful individuals from outside the community.[5] Also Muslim potentates were sometimes active in appointments (Ovadia 5).

The crucial common element in the public appointments in mellah society was that they adhered to the principle of serara, patrilineal inheritance (literally, "government"). The people of the mellah were primarily concerned that the hereditary rights of scholars be preserved, provided that the candidates involved had the personal qualifications for the positions they sought. Given the two factors of inheritance and qualifications, people were only secondarily concerned with the details of the mechanism of appointment, though appointment by sages was preferred. The widespread application of the principle of appointment, from only within a strictly delimited pool of lawful candidates, is much in evidence in the communities. The leading sages of the communities are predominantly members of a small number of families. The same names recur generation after generation in the same communities. Thus the Toledano-Berdugo family dominated the Meknes rabbinate for hundreds of years; the Elbaz, Abitbul, and Ben-Hamu families that of Sefrou. Probably the extreme case is that of Fez where the Sarfati and Ibn-Danan families predominated. The latter constitute a virtually unbroken chain that extends from the fourteenth century until well into the twentieth century.[6] These rabbinical lineages are, occasionally and temporarily, interrupted only when the family does not produce a suitable candidate. Thereafter, when such a candidate does emerge, a dispute typically erupts between the descendant of the substitute and the scion of the old family.

The serara principle governed many minor public functions besides the important one of judge. Thus, the sages of the Elbaz family in Sefrou had the hereditary right to engage in writing marriage contracts (ketubot) and to assess the value of dowries (Ovadia 1975–1985, vol. 3: 47). Elsewhere we hear of "the serara of marriage contracts and divorce bills" (Ya'aqov Berdugo, Even ha'ezer 48). The deeply rooted principle of hereditary positions was founded on the notion of "privilege of ancestors" (zekhut avot), which was considered to be the right of latter-day descendants. The principle is not original in Moroccan Jewry but figures in classical halakhic sources, particularly in the twelfth-century codex of Maimonides. In their legal discussions, the sages of our period invariably refer to the Talmudic and medieval sources to back their support of hereditary claims. The crucial point is that these sources were available to the sages of traditional Jewry in all times and places, but the sages of Morocco in particular placed unique emphasis on them, considering them relevant to the problems of their society and extended their application creatively. The potency of the "privilege of ancestors" principle led to great self-confidence. Thus we encounter an eighteenth-century Meknes judge of the Toledano family who appointed three judges to follow him. Of the three, one was his own son, another a cousin, and the third a member of the Berdugo family that was intertwined with the Toledanos (Bar-Asher 1981: 101–102).

The regular availability of suitable candidates, for rabbinical and judicial positions, from within select family circles, was linked to the system of schooling. At the elementary level schooling was largely universal, based on the entrepreneurial initiative of teachers and on the payment ability of parents. At the higher level, however, only select youths obtained schooling, and teaching was organized within family settings. Typically, a sage taught a small, select group of students, who were primarily of his family. The letter of a young man to a sage, pleading to permit him to come and to be accepted for studies, is illuminating. He requests of the sage "to read with [you] nightly the *Yoreh dei'a* laws, or anything your honor wishes." Rather movingly the writer supports his request with the argument, "for you are of our flesh and our brother" (Ovadia 658). Conceivably, such a request could also have been bolstered by many other arguments. In the Jewish context in particular, pious reference might have been made to the worthiness of studying the holy Torah, but apparently the familial argument was closest to the heart of the writer, and presumably also to that of the recipient of the message. As such students matured, they became candidates for rabbinical positions. For this to materialize, the candidates had to master learning and to exhibit the personal qualities considered appropriate for the position. It remained for senior sages to attest to the qualifications of a particular candidate, and those were usually his teachers, who were also his kinsmen.

The aforementioned dispute around Abitbul illustrates the operation of some elements of the system. The lay opponents of Abitbul sought to appoint another judge and thus to dislodge Abitbul from his position as judge. In one of their messages, the Sefrou people claimed that their initiative was founded upon "the will of the sages" (Ovadia 137), but they did not name them. Had any sages actually approved of the initiative, the activists would have served themselves well by publicizing the details, identities included. The fact that they did not do so probably indicates that, in fact, there were no such sages. Furthermore, the statement of the Sefrou people demonstrates that they considered it important to legitimize their doings by claiming that they had the backing of sages. It is not enough, then, in Moroccan Jewry that the people of the community elect their sage; the act also requires the approval of other sages.

The documents of the Abitful case include a remarkable letter by his teacher, Rabbi Eliyahu Sarfati, the senior sage of Fez at the time, to "the nagid and individuals" of Sefrou. Sarfati writes about his protégé as follows:

> Do you perhaps think that it was you who authorized him to be a judge (*semakhtem oto le'dayan*) . . . ? It was I who authorized him to be a judge, and my authorization is under his hand! . . . Against your will shall he adjudicate you [all], the little ones and the great . . . I want you to go the way of the previous generation, that obeyed the sages . . . And the city of Sefrou had the best reputation of all the surrounding cities. But you—you go the other way! . . . [Therefore] if you want to depose him—even if he agrees, I shall object! (Ovadia 9)

The note of absolute authority and assertivity, of the sage of the neighboring community, is founded on his having authorized the sage in question. This brings us to the issue of the relationship between "authorization," as it figures in this source, and "appointment." Evidently, Sarfati does not discern between the two terms; to him authorization implies appointment to a specific position. This lack of differentiation also emerges from a letter that Abitbul had sent to his old teacher, at an earlier time when the relations with his community had been happier. Abitbul writes:

> Rest your hand (*semokh yadkha*) on me, and [then] I will never lack anything . . . [For] when the community made me (*he'emisu alai*) prayer leader to serve in sanctity, I accepted only upon the condition [that] you would agree. (Ovadia 19)

Abitbol evidently felt, that his appointment was improper without the "resting of hand" (*semikha*), authorization, on the part of his teacher. Thereupon, Sarfati indeed sent a letter of authorization to Abitbul, formulated in the standard terms of rabbinical entitlement (*yoreh yoreh yadin yadin*) (Ovadia 19).

These sources indicate, first, that in rabbinical appointments the role of sages, even ousiders, was clearly superior to that of lay individuals of the local community. Second, that authorization was part and parcel of the act of appointment, though it might follow appointment, legitimizing one that was otherwise improper. People did not conceive of authorization as an independent action that might precede appointment to a particular position. This constitutes a social situation different from that of more highly formalized institutions (such as the medieval university system in Europe, and the Ashkenazic rabbinical training system that parallels it). When scholars attained positions in Moroccan communities, superior sages, their teachers in particular, used to give them letters of authorization. Such documents were not issued independently of an appointment procedure. Authorization papers were never issued without the specific address of community governors who were engaged in the process of appointing the bearer of the authorization. Anonymous documents, in terms of "to whom it may concern" (such as were issued in Ashkenazic Jewry), were completely foreign to precolonial Morocco.[7]

There were not very many rabbinical families in eighteenth- and nineteenth-century Morocco. The families that were there were deeply entrenched in their home communities and functioned there generation after generation. As a young scholar approached maturity and the termination of his studies, he did not expose himself to an open market for rabbinical candidates. Rather he awaited a specific position to become available to him. Such a position would come to him as an inheritance from a senior family member, who functioned either as a superior sage in a court of law, or as an ordinary sage (such as court scribe, synagogue leader, ritual slaughterer). As the eventuality of a position materialized, the young sage was appointed by the individuals of the community and authorized by his teachers or other rabbinical superiors.[8] The acts of authorization and appointment are thus undifferentiated. We find even the haughty Sarfati saying that the authorization of Abitbul was given "in agreement with the people of the community" (be'haskamat benei ha'qehilla) (Ovadia 19).

This is the background to Sarfati's authoritarian attitude toward the Sefrou laymen. Evidently, Sarfati felt that the act of appointment was integral to the act of authorization, and he was entitled to involvement in both. The weak response of the Sefrou laymen, vaguely referring to sages who supported them, expresses their position in the dispute, which does not differ in essence from his. They do not dispute Sarfati's claim on principle. Rather, within a context of sage–lay relationships to which all acquiesce, the Sefrou elders take the side of one sage against another. The case reflects also the salience of the element of personality in the rabbinical role. In asserting his position, Sarfati bases himself on his dominant personality no less, and perhaps even more, than on any abstract rules.

The salience of the personal factor is also evident in the case that follows. The judges of Fez were called upon to adjudicate the case of a small community in the late eighteenth century (apparently again Sefrou) that used to have a court composed of a single judge only. In time, more judges had been appointed, and the individuals, jointly with these sages, had decided that a quorum of three judges was henceforth required. The question that came before the Fez court concerned the authority of the original judge: Would he henceforth have to operate with the other judges, or could he continue to adjudicate by himself as he had in the past? The court decided that, indeed, his rights were valid, and they compromised, leaving certain areas that could be adjudicated by him alone (S. Y. Abitbul, vol. 2, 88). The mere raising of the possibility of the rights of the individual judge under these circumstances is remarkable, all the more so the support that the court gave him against the community. Ibn-Sur (262) also adjudicated such a case. The implication of these decisions is that the authority of the individual judge is not anchored only, and perhaps not even primarily, in the institution of the court of law in which he fills a role. Authority is invested in him as an individual person. Therefore, a later change in the structure of the institution that pertains to him, the enlargement of the quorum of the court of law from one to three, affects him only partially.

The term by which judges were referred to reflects this situation. The precise term for the role of judge is *dayan,* but we also encounter the term *beit din* (court of law) used to refer to an individual judge (Ibn-Sur 143). A particular sage is thus considered to be congruent with an institution; the latter becomes part of his person. This terminology expresses the emphasis of Moroccan society upon the weight of individuals, as against the lesser importance that is attributed to formal institutions.[9]

The limited extent to which social roles and institutions were formalized emerges also as we turn to the question of the area of jurisdiction of the courts of law. This was altogether vague. Frequently, after the delivery of judgment, a plaintiff would appeal to another court, elsewhere, and the latter would offer an opinion (Ovadia 1975–1985, vol. 3: 71; Ibn-Sur 262). We hear of a litigant who refuses to be adjudicated by the court of his town (Ovadia 123). We also encounter a case of litigants who came to a complex agreement, that their dispute be heard separately by the three courts of Fez, Meknes, and Sefrou, and that they would abide by the judgment of the majority of the courts (Ovadia 643). In Chapter 2 we encountered a litigant who refused to appear before a certain court.

Probably because of the potential for disorder inherent in such a case, we encounter attempts on the part of judges to limit the freedom of litigants in seeking justice. One sage, Rabbi Refael Moshe Elbaz, declared that after delivery of judgment the litigants would be permitted to present their case before another court, but the first court would not be obliged to abide by the judgment of the second court (R. M. Elbaz, Hoshen mishpat 140). Another sage, Rabbi Yoseif Berdugo, declared, that litigants would be permitted to present their case to another court if the first court was presided over by only one or two judges. But he forbade this if the first court was composed of a full complement of three judges (Yoseif Berdugo I, 1922–1943: 34b).

In actuality, however, the authority of courts was not delimited in such ways. The aforementioned Berdugo comments feebly about his opinion on the right of appeal:

And this is the accepted view among all early and late codifiers. But in our times I have not seen [anyone] concerned about that, and [they cause] disputes to increase in Israel. May God forgive them.

One particular case ran the following convoluted course. A litigant named Avraham was sued by one Yoseif, for a sum of money, before the Fez court. The court found that he was liable for payment. Thereupon, Avraham brought his case before the Sefrou court. That court considered the matter and acquiesced with the Fez judgment. Avraham then turned to the Meknes court which supported him, disagreeing with the previous decisions. As a result, the Fez court reconsidered its judgment and suggested a compromise between the litigants, thus lessening the sum to be paid by Avraham. The court also decided that it would hold a separate deliberation regarding the balance. In the Fez court's second decision the judge expressed himself as follows:

> Hence I acquiesce to the said R. Avraham's request, and declare that R. Yoseif may not seize (le'aqeil) anything, until he provides a contradiction (setirah) to the judgment that I have written. (Ibn-Sur 7)

The mildness of this judge, whose authority was assailed from several directions, is remarkable. His judgment even implies the possibility that it might be challenged again in the future. Indeed, the data we have on hand does not reflect the final resolution of the matter.

How, then, is the scope of authority of the Moroccan Jewish court delimited, and where is the source of its authority? A Tetuan source affords an insight:

> If a judge is accepted as such in the town, and rules justly—he has been sanctified (qideshuhu) by Heaven . . . one is not permitted to present the claim before another court. (Ben-Walid, vol. 2, 16)

The sage goes on to say that if, however, other sages challenge such a judge's decision, the litigants are permitted to present their claim to another court. (But other sages would not initially be in a position to know of the case had not one of the litigants brought it to their attention in the first place; hence the proviso is immaterial). Crucially, however, the sage concludes that if the litigants agreed under oath to accept the judgment of a particular judge, "then that judge becomes like a court of seventy-one [judges]." This idiom refers to the prototypical rabbinical court of Temple times, whose standing had an aura of sanctity and ultimacy. The source of judicial authority that emerges from these statements is clearly, then, not appointment to the judicial office in general. It is, rather, the particular appointment of a judge on the part of litigants (in the form of an oath taking) to adjudicate a specific case, which entails the most binding judicial authority in Moroccan Jewry.

We turn now to the question as to how the sages maintained themselves. The ideal was that the community would earmark a portion of the income of a public synagogue, such as a third or a quarter, for a particular sage. The donations of worshippers to their synagogues did not have the attribute of a lowly charity but rather of sacrament. They were earmarked as being "in honor of the Torah" (*likhvod ha'torah*), namely, for the sage who personified holy learning. A Fez sage, writing about a Sefrou synagogue dispute, expressed this ideal as follows:

> The order of things, ever since creation, has changed . . . In the past [people] used to give the judges the income of public synagogues, so that they should benefit from them. Indeed the descendants [of those judges] still benefit from them to this day. But [in the present case the people] did not give the sage any portion of the income of the public synagogue. They do worse: they take away [from him] . . . they extract the sacred, and implant it in the realm of defilement (*mosi'im ha'qedusha ve'notenim ota le'sitra ahra*). (Ovadia 5)

The powerful, virtually demonic, *sitra ahra* idiom, is commonly used to refer to whatever is antithetic to godliness. In the conception of mellah people, the proper way of supporting a sage is not by giving him a salary but by affording him an unspecified income that is embedded in holy services. Withholding such income from its due recipient, and using it for another purpose, entails channeling it to secularity, hence defilement.

Also, in actuality, we find that sages commonly lived on the income of synagogues. The sources of the period are replete with cases revolving on the rights of sages to this source of income, and in the chapter on synagogues (Chap. 7) we discuss the matter at length. During the course of our period, particularly in the nineteenth century, many sages came to have their own private synagogues, and the donations of the worshippers served as their income. The opening of private synagogues by sages was a recurring cause of dispute, because it led some worshippers to remove themselves from existing synagogues, causing affront to the sages of those synagogues and diminishing their source of income. This problem in time became so aggravated that during the colonial period there operated a court of law that specialized in synagogue disputes between sages.[10] In practice there was not much difference between the public and the private synagogues in respect to the income of the sages who managed them. Rabbinical positions were commonly inherited, and the income of synagogues also was inherited. Therefore, neither type of synagogue was controlled by their congregations.

The ranking sages, the judges, also maintained themselves by drawing payment from the litigants, paid, of course, in strictly equal sums and before delivery of judgment. Maintenance of judges by the payment of a salary does not seem to have been conceivable in precolonial times.[11] Only in the case of sages of low rank (such as the synagogue leader of a small community mentioned in Chap. 4) are there rare indications that a salary was paid. Besides the preference of people to support ranking sages out of hallowed funds, there was also a practical difficulty in paying a salary, since the communities had no well-institutionalized treasuries. They did on occasion have a "chest for the poor" (*qupat sedaqa*), out of which, in theory, a salary could have been paid. But, in fact, that would have been virtually insulting and occurred only in cases of dire need (Ben-Malka 106). Sometimes we hear that judges were given supplementary support out of "public sources" (*mi'shel sibbur*) (Ibn-Sur 47; Ben-Naim: 64b).

In general, the sages seem to have abhorred any support that had the tinge of charity. A striking indication of this emerges in a sermon about the ideal qualities of the Torah sage, in which figures a homiletic interpretation of the verse, "And a menstruating woman he did not approach" (Ezek. 18.6). "That," explained the preacher, "refers to a sage who refrains from benefitting from charity!" (M. Toledano: 56b). The preacher associates accepting charity with the ultimate of defilement in traditional sensitivity. The homily reflects a situation where dignified sages avoided acceptance of overt charity, but when driven by need they did sometimes enjoy other forms of material support from the public.

We also encounter, particularly in Sefrou, sages who supported themselves by ordinary business ventures (Ovadia 129, 505, 514, 541). We hear of legal complications in which these sages became involved, as a result of their routine business dealings with laymen in their communities. An important indication of the dimension of some of the sages' business affairs is the fact that sometimes their communities owed them money (Ovadia 107, 206, 231; 1975–1985, vol. 4, 37). One reason for such debts is that sometimes the sage-businessman paid taxes and extortions on behalf of the community to the local potentates, when the latter considered the sage to be in a position to deliver payment (Ovadia 152). Moreover, we hear of sages who were incarcerated by Muslim potentates, presumably because their wealth aroused greed, and/or because they were perceived as representatives of their communities. Remarkably, in some cases these sages extricated themselves by funding their redemption out of their own resources (Ovadia 1, also 301). Most of these data stem from Sefrou during a relatively short period of two decades around 1800, and this reflects the considerable resources that these sages must have commanded. [12]

The social condition that permitted economic competition between sages and laymen (and hence litigations involving the two categories of people) is of sociological import. That condition is the imperfect formalization of political roles in the political system of the mellah. Thus, the roles of judges, and of sages in general, are not closely defined and differentiated from those of ordinary people in the community. Supporting the sages by the payment of a regular communal salary could have bolstered the formalization of their position and could have inhibited them from engaging in business. But Moroccan Jewry during our period did not develop such a practice. [13]

The role of *shoheit*, ritual slaughterer, is not as politically and socially prominent as are other rabbinical roles. It is, nevertheless, an important role in the context of daily domestic life. The information on hand about the structure of the role of shoheit leads to a picture of greater formalization than that of judge. As distinct from the latter appointment, the role of shoheit was not unambiguously governed by inheritance laws. While the sages were unanimous about the application of inheritance rules to the role of judge, they vacillated when facing disputes of appointments to the role of shoheit. They maintained that on principle ritual slaughtering was not governed by serara rules, but that according to local custom the rules did apply (Yoseif Berdugo I, 1974: 85; Ben-Walid, vol. 2, 104).

The relative openness of the role of shoheit to outsiders necessitated a measure of public control that we do not encounter in any other rabbinical activity. A regulation of the Fez sages reads as follows:

> Not just anyone may declare himself to be a shoheit; only the shohatim of the slaughter house (*maqolim*) may do so. Besides them no one may raise his hand, even if he be an expert. Except

if he consults with us and we agree. Otherwise we shall declare his slaughtering to be like slaughtering by a gentile. (Seifer ha' taqanot 138)

These legislators recognized the possibility of there being "expertise" in the field of slaughtering that is not certified by the sages. Indeed, the sources contain several authorizations for the role of shoheit (Ovadia, 13, 19, 481, 490), such as is requested by the regulation. The authorizations for slaughtering, known by a special term, *qabala,* were general and were not issued for the purpose of attaining a particular position. The role of shoheit was not strictly enclosed and controlled by rabbinical families, and therefore elements of impersonal control, such as qabala documents and a specific regulation, as that of Fez, served to prevent disorder in this particular ritual practice. Sometimes, as we saw in the case discussed in Chapter 4, slaughterers made a living by receiving a salary from the community. But much more commonly they were paid by the individuals who sought their services, as the occasion arose. The appointment of a shoheit to a position only entailed obtaining permission or the right to exercise the skill. Given the differences between them, the conditions of livelihood of both judges and ritual slaughterers reflect the low extent of institutionalization of public roles in mellah society.

We are now in a position to attempt a comparative summary. The standing of Moroccan rabbis is rooted primarily in the social milieus of private synagogues, and only secondarily in communitywide institutions that span the social circles and individuals who compose the society of the mellah. This secondary source of authority also is important, but it is not consistently developed, only partially institutionalized. The power of Moroccan sages lies in their mastery over concrete organizations and social groups, private synagogues that constitute only a part of the society of the mellah. Sometimes the power of sages also lies in their mastery of particular roles, such as that of judge, as a result of hereditary rights, and occasionally the sages governed without any overt concern for public support, as we saw in the intervention of Sarfati in favor of his disciple Abitbul. The summary picture is one of a leadership whose social base is not very broad.

This leads us to question the source of power of these sages who filled such active roles in community politics. Where does a sage such as Sarfati draw the self-assurance to act authoritatively in the secular doings of people who are not bound to him by any institutional ties?

I approach the question by considering the terms of respect that people used in reference to their religious leaders. We have on hand hundreds of letters that were addressed to sages by their colleagues, and sometimes by laymen. These letters are replete with florid and fanciful baroque-style praise of the sages to whom they are written.[14] Remarkably, however, in contrast to the style of their Ashkenazic contemporaries, the Moroccan writers do not praise the judges in terms of the important positions they hold, nor in terms of the great communities that they serve. This is particularly remarkable in view of the sensitivity of people for their localities, as we saw in Chapter 3.

The element that figures most prominently as the sages legitimize themselves in their writings is that of lineage. We encounter expressions such as "the Torah is their inheritance from their ancestors, generation after generation" (Monsoniego 11). One sage is referred to as "a descendant of the great and famous rabbi, the honorable one, our teacher and master, the rabbi . . ." (Ovadia 334). The authors and publishers of books offer details of their lineage in the prefaces (Y. Ibn-Danan; A. Elbaz). A sage, writing of the tribulations that befell him, expresses himself, "the merit of my holy ancestors supported me" (Ben-Malka 84). In letters of petition by and on behalf of needy sages, we encounter the same motif. Thus: "and act for us and for our holy ancestors" (Ovadia 145, 131). In a letter of complaint about a sage whom the addressee had insulted, we find the following argument: "and you did not care for his honor and the honor of his holy ancestors!" (Ovadia 340). And in another epistle of this kind: ". . . and besides . . . he is a descendant of the mighty ones, those of great force—those who fulfill God's word! Certainly anyone who merely touches upon his means of livelihood . . . will not depart this world in peace!" (M. Toledano: 56b). In recommendations for itinerant beggars, mention is frequently made of their worthy ancestors. For instance: "Take care of him, [both] for his honor and for that of his ancestors, may their memory in paradise be a blessing" (Ovadia 575b; also 351, 354). A sage writing to a wayward husband, warning him not to desert his wife, again uses the ancestral motif: "for she is a descendant of holy ones" (Ovadia 128).

In a late nineteenth-century source we encounter a development of the ancestral motif. After mentioning the beneficiary's righteous ancestors, in a letter of recommendation on behalf of a needy scholar, the writer adds, "And further, after his decease . . . he [the beneficiary] will be steadfast to save you in times of misfortune" (Ovadia 196).

People indeed visited the burial places of deceased sages to pray there in times of exceptional need. The custom of visiting such sites led to the practice, documented in the case of Fez, of burying sages in a separate section of the local cemetery. This was named *Hevron,* after the hallowed burial place of the biblical patriarchs in the Holy Land in Hebron (Ovadia 1979, French section: 57).

There is an indication from Meknes in the second quarter of the nineteenth century that the veneration of saints had legal import. The community was being disturbed by an unknown thief. Thereupon a time-honored practice was put into effect: in the synagogue the sages declared the thief excommunicated if he did not promptly return his spoils. But that had no effect. The sages repeated their declaration, not in the synagogue but "at the tomb of the saint" (*qever ha'saddiq*), and thereupon a man presented himself with the stolen goods (Yoseif Berdugo I, 1922–1943, vol. 2: 10b). We do not know the identity of the particular saint whose involvement had such dramatic effect, but the phrase "the tomb of the saint" with the definite article indicates the practice to have been well established, requiring no further explanation. From the same source we hear of a practice in connection with saint veneration. A man wore on his person, as a prophylactic, a golden coin that had been placed on a saintly tomb (*she'manihim al qivrot ha'saddiqim*). Again, the particular Hebrew turn of phrase, in the present continuous, indicates that the practice was well-established (Yoseif Berdugo I, 1922–1943; 28a).

The second half of the nineteenth century was apparently a turning point in the development of saint veneration. Whereas indications during the early part of the century show evidence only of folk practice, we now have evidence of the incorporation of the practices in formal rabbinical legislation. A Meknes sage, Rabbi Hayim Meshash (d. 1904), writing about the obligations of a husband to his spouse in case of illness, offers a striking testimony:

> . . . and in the generation before us [the sages] further added an obligation [on the husband] to take her on pilgrimage (*le'holikha le'hishtateiah*) to the graves of the pious ones (may their merit guard us), [even] in another city . . . and the rabbis of Fez and Sefrou disputed this . . . But amongst us it is common practice to oblige the husband [to do so]. (H. Meshash: 234)

This testimony shows that saint veneration was developing in the late nineteenth century and that it was controversial. The Fez and Sefrou sages opposed burdening the husband with visits to distant sites, while in Meknes the veneration of saints developed more radically.[15]

The conception that the sages had of themselves and their view in the eyes of laymen is of sociological import. It offers an answer to the question of the source of their authority and actual power. The domineering presence of a Fez sage such as Rabbi Eliyahu Sarfati vis-à-vis the people of Sefrou lies in sages being conceived as lofty personalities, above ordinary men. The sages are also conceived as carrying *zekhut avot*, "the merit of ancestors," who even in the remote past were all "inheritors of the Torah." There are indications that the self-conception of sages underwent changes in the nineteenth century parallel to the development of saint veneration. Again from a Meknes sage, we have on hand a pertinent discussion of the various sanctions to be meted out in retribution for verbal insults, such as calling a person a whore, a boor, and so forth. These are mostly excommunication (*niduy*) and lashing (*malqot*). Remarkably, the sage differentiates between an offender who is a layman (*'am ha'ares*) and an offender who is a sage (*talmid hakham*). He writes:

> The rule we have on hand by Rav Sherira Gaon, that whoever shames another one is excommunicated—that applies to incidents involving equals. But Heaven forbid to excommunicate a sage who shamed a layman. This I said out of reasoning (*mi'sevara*). (Yoseif Berdugo I, 1922–1943: 41b)

The sage refers to the ruling of a major tenth-century Babylonian master, but it is extraordinary that he qualifies that ruling by his own consideration. Such a qualification in rabbinical tradition normally requires marshaling the support of weighty authorities. The Meknes sage, however, felt so strongly on this point that he bypassed the traditional procedure. He sought no support in the sources and based himself only on his solitary deliberation.[16]

The conception of the sage in Moroccan Jewry as *saddiq*, saint, has some elements in common with the parallel conception of the marabout among Moroccan Muslims. Stillman (1982) has summarized the common and disparate characteristics of saint and marabout. In both cases the elements of personality and ancestry are salient to the believers. But in contrast to the marabout, the saint causes fewer miracles in his lifetime, his physical person is not considered as power laden as that of the marabout, and he does not usually become legendary in his lifetime. In our own times, the colonial and postcolonial periods, there is a great flowering of marabout-type elements among Moroccan Jews, both in Morocco and in their new places of settlement.[17]

Judeo-Moroccan religious leadership of Sherifian times is characterized by hereditary charisma.[18] The sages do not attain respect primarily because of their formal roles and positions. The scholarly and personal writings of the sages indeed demonstrate their great learning and their lofty moral personalities. Excellence in scholarship and extraordinary piety, however, do not figure as important in the mutual relationships of the sages as reflected by contemporary sources. Scholarship and piety also figure second only in the Moroccan-Jewish hagiography that we have on hand. Rather, in the popular memory, as enshrined in the works collated by the folklorists, there predominates the motif of the saint, who graced with ancestral merit overcomes miraculously his rude adversaries (Noy 1964). This feature of the sage constitutes saintliness in the Moroccan-Jewish conception and is the source of spiritual power. The power of saintliness enabled the sages to participate in the government of their communities, despite the weakness of their position in terms of the formal social structure. Thus, having uncovered the nature of the standing of the sages vis-à-vis other community potentates, we are now in a position to focus, in the next chapter, on the sages at home, in their own synagogue milieus.

7   RELIGIOUS LIFE:
THE SYNAGOGUES

The synagogues were the core arena of religiosity in the mellahs. Having in previous chapters seen the sages active in the secular domain, we turn now to the synagogues to observe the sages and their contemporaries in their religious doings. The synagogues in traditional Jewish societies fill a weighty social role. Important activities in the area of religion, internal politics, scholarly learning, aesthetic creativity, charity—all take place in the synagogue. Beyond this very general observation, however, there are significant differences in detail and emphasis between the synagogues of various Jewish societies. Synagogue-related matters figure frequently in the rabbinical sources of Sherifian times. Accepted wisdom about traditional Jewry also accords the synagogues much importance. Given this background, it is tempting to exaggerate the salience of synagogues in the actual lives of people. But we want to uncover a balanced picture regarding the roles that synagogues did and did not fill in mellah society. In this chapter, I seek to uncover the particular features of synagogues in Sherifian times and contribute thereby to a sociology of synagogues.[1]

Torah learning is a matter of great weight in Judaism. I begin, therefore, with an examination of the role of mellah synagogues in the area of scholarship. In contrast to the practice of certain other Jewish societies (such as the Yemen and many parts of Eastern Europe), the mellah synagogues were not the most important venues for Torah learning.[2] People also learned at home in family settings. The main scholarly activity that did take place in synagogues was the frequent delivery of derashot-type lectures by sages. These were wide-ranging discourses of biblical homiletics, practical halakha, and general rabbinic learning. The delivery of such lectures, particularly on the Sabbath, was part of the regular duties of sages in synagogues. The audience was normally passive at the derashot, and books were not used.

Those were rare and valuable, and people kept them at home among their treasured possessions. We hear of a sage who, upon obtaining new books, is apprehensive of the fact becoming common knowledge. He worries that other scholars will importune him with requests to borrow the precious volumes, which might then suffer from wear and tear.[3]

The sacredness attributed to synagogues also inhibited their use as schools for children. That was usually done in the private homes of the teachers or in premises that the teachers rented for the purpose. But teachers often had difficulties finding premises for their work. The presence of school children was generally considered a nuisance, particularly because of the very limited toilet facilities that could not accommodate large numbers of people in a civilized fashion. Also, the noise was disturbing where people normally lived in crowded apartments that all faced a central courtyard. It is typical that a sage considered it appropriate to single out a synagogue community for praise, for having permitted a teacher to operate on its premises (Ben-Malka 106).[4] Further, there are indications that private homes served not only as places of learning but also for mystic activities that are at the core of the sacred, namely, the ritual reading of the *Zohar* book (Stahl 1979b),[5] an activity one might have expected to take place in sacred synagogue territory only.

Specialized study groups were, however, sometimes located in the synagogues. In eighteenth-century Fez we hear of a *hevrat hesgeir*, literally "association of the enclosed" (more probably, "the sedentary"). This was a group of men who devoted time to Torah studies and obtained material support from others. We may presume that such a formally organized group of scholars used a synagogue as their venue. It is remarkable that our knowledge of the existence of this eighteenth-century Fez group comes from the fact that the neighboring communities of Meknes and Sefrou received appeals to support them (Ovadia 1979, vol. 2: 367–369). This indicates that those communities probably did not maintain a comparable group of scholars, for otherwise there would have been little point in turning to them for support. The Fez "association of the sedentary" was thus probably a rarity. In the middle of the nineteenth century we hear of another such institution in Fez: a wealthy individual purchased books and encouraged scholars through his material support to use them (A. Anqawe 36).

We have a report of a study group (*yeshiva*) that was active in Sefrou at the end of the century for a period of nine years. The group comprised ten scholars who studied the Talmud and legists (*posqim*) for three hours every morning. Six of the men were "great rabbis," and three were "students who had not yet finished their studies." The latter also studied ritual slaughtering with the former. They all received a small monthly stipend from the benefactor who had initiated the group, the students receiving one-quarter less than the rabbis. At first the group functioned in a synagogue. Later it moved to

> the great study-house (*beit midrash*) of the rabbis, Rabbi Sha'ul Yeshu'a Abitbul and Rabbi Amor his son, that was closed for many years, and was full of books. (Y. Ovadia: 25–27; also Ovadia 75)

The group thus moved from a public facility into the library of a private family, the Abitbuls, an ancient rabbinical family that had been active in Sefrou in the past but in the course of the nineteenth century had produced no scholars to use its books. This development of the Sefrou yeshiva reflects the powerful hold of the individual domain over that of public institutions.[6]

The holding of prayers, religious services in the restricted sense of the term, was of course another major synagogue function. In Moroccan Jewry religious services were elaborately embellished by additional chants and hymns (*piyutim*) that permitted the differential participation of many individuals. This endowed the religious services of Moroccan Jewry with aesthetic additions to a larger extent than other Jewish societies. An appreciation of this element of mellah synagogue activity is essential for an understanding of the culture of the people who frequented the synagogues. But to date the information available to us on the sociology of the synagogue arts of Morocco is very limited.[7] Popular participation in religious services in the communities was thus bolstered, not only by religiosity and the associated underpinnings of social control but also by aesthetic appeal and the scope that this offered for individual expression.

Given this background, it is notable that the synagogues saw the full attendance of their congregations only at the major seasonal holy days, not on the Sabbath, and certainly not on weekdays. The communities were subject to the socioeconomic conditions described above (in Chap. 3). An important characteristic of these was the dispersion of numerous people, who worked by traveling among distant and widely spread tribesmen. In the sources we hear pronouncements of the sages, in connection with synagogue affairs, that echo those con-

ditions. Thus, a sage preaching to his congregation about the obligation to attend daily morning services makes allowance "for whoever
must travel urgently, or is otherwise pressed because he is needy" (Ovadia 90). (The sage does not note that such a person must say his prayers in private, that being understood.) Another sage, writing about
the virtues of a bridegroom, mentions that he comes to the synagogue
daily for both the morning and evening services (Ovadia 97). Such
praise is naturally appropriate only where many people do not act as
virtuously. Even on the Sabbath many people were absent from synagogue. The turn of phrase of a Meknes sage is illuminating in this
context. Writing about matters unrelated to religion, he mentions as
a matter of course:

> . . . on Sabbath when all the community is not gathered together
> to pray, because of course some of them (she'harey yeish meihem) are
> in the tents of Qeidar [Berbers] . . . (Yoseif Berdugo II, 1972:
> 170)[8]

The fact that people were away from their homes for extended periods
was an accepted fact of life. The scope of peddling was so wide that
the complete congregation of people in the synagogue perforce took
place on the major holy days only.

The most characteristic feature of the mellah synagogues was that
they were managed by sages as if they were their private property.
Indeed, many synagogues actually were private property of the sages.
But, significantly, with regard to management there were not many
differences between the various synagogues, despite differences in the
types of formal ownership. The management of mellah synagogues was
usually governed by particular inheritance laws that pertained to public offices (diney serara). According to these laws, synagogues were
managed at the personal discretion of the sage who inherited his synagogue position. There were several types of ownership of synagogues,
the differences, however, as we shall see, affected synagogue management only marginally.

One type of ownership was "of the community" (shel sibbur). Such
synagogues had been founded in the past by communities, and the
individuals of the community had appointed a sage to manage them.[9]
In the times that concern us, the eighteenth and nineteenth centuries,
the community-owned synagogues were not managed by the public
but by sages who were the descendants of the sages of the past.[10] The
inheritors received the voluntary gifts of the public to the synagogue,

and payments for purchasing synagogue honors (misvot). These moneys provided the sages with a livelihood. The latter for their part were responsible for the physical maintenance of the facility, besides offering their professional religious and cultural services. The sages, in the words of a nineteenth-century Meknes sage, were,

> to gather the community, and to be their messenger [to God] and pray; to expound the religious laws to them . . .; to guide them, and cause them to go the right way. (Ya'aqov Berdugo, Yoreh dei'a 6)

The sage who inherited his position in a community-owned synagogue was in fact in an independent position. His status vis-à-vis the congregants was, as this authority phrased it trenchantly, that of "one who invites them to his house." Further, Berdugo ruled, the payments of the congregants to the sage of such a synagogue were not to be earmarked for the maintenance of the facility. For that, he emphasized, is the responsibility of the sage and not of the congregation. We thus conclude that the payments of the congregants to the synagogue are of a diffuse nature, for the synagogue sage, in all aspects of his person and public activities—as a patrimonial host.[11]

The salient public element in the community-owned synagogues, that was of practical effect, was the following: sometimes a portion of the income of these synagogues was used for the succor of the needy. This portion might amount to a third or even half the total income of the synagogue (Ovadia 98, 108). As to the remaining portions of the synagogue income, it would be said in the terminology of the times that "Rabbi so-and-so has *serara,* rule over them." Frequently those portions were divided among several sages, descendants of the sage who had originally been appointed to the position. Because of the possibility of sharing serara among sages, the holders of serara feared the claims of rivals to their inheritances. There was much scope for disputes among the sages, and between sages and laymen supporting protagonists.

A second type of synagogue ownership was "of owners" (*shel be'alim*), or "of individuals" (*shel yehidim*). The practical difference between these and community-owned synagogues was that in the individually owned ones usually no portion of the income was earmarked for the needy. Also, the individually owned synagogues were managed by sages on the basis of serara inheritance. Such a synagogue might have been founded by a sage and managed by his scholarly descendants. Or it might have been founded by a powerful layman who had then hired a sage to manage it, and the descendants of that sage then enjoyed ser-ara. Such private synagogues must have been very common, for people had the conception that all synagogues were of this type. We hear the following statement repeatedly by eighteenth-century Tetuan and Meknes sages:

> At this time all our synagogues are of individuals, and not of the community or of endowment. (Ben-Malka 25; Ya'aqov Berdugo, Hoshen mishpat 17; M. Toledano: 56b)

The statement is exaggerated, and probably reflects the objection of these sages to a situation they deplored but were unable to change. The attitude of the sages to the phenomenon of privately owned syn-agogues is clearly negative. Their preference is for community-owned synagogues managed by hereditary sages, whose positions are not en-dangered by people who might open rival synagogues. During the early part of our period we find the sages consistently opposing at-tempts to establish new synagogues. During the nineteenth century, however, the sages falter, and eventually resign themselves to indis-criminate opening of synagogues. They even change their theoretical-legal view of the matter.

The initial negative position of the sages, as well as some of the passions that motivated people to establish new synagogues, are well reflected in the following Sefrou case that began in the late seventeenth century. In the past there had been in the then small community only one synagogue, owned by the community and managed by hereditary sages. Later, two new synagogues had been founded upon the initiative of the "majority of the community." Because of the splitting of the community into three congregations, the income of the sages of the old synagogue had fallen, and this grievance they took to the sages of Fez. The heads of the new synagogues offered to remunerate the loss of the sages of the old synagogue by paying them a stipend out of community funds. To this the Fez sages reacted indignantly:

> [You] take away from them what is theirs and [was] their fathers' . . . and you [suggest] maintaining them out of community [funds] (mi'shel sibbur)!? [That] we have not [ever] heard! By this we mean: it is unreasonable!

They go on to berate the Sefrou people:

> They [seek] to make themselves grand and magnificent, to make a reputation for themselves by appointing a prayer-leader of their

choice, and by having a synagogue called by their name. And all
their intention is to diminish the income of . . . the [other] synagogues! (Ovadia 11)

The salient motive in the sages' position was material: they were
concerned that the income of the spiritual leaders of the community
be secure. They were also concerned that community institutions function in an orderly manner. Another consideration was that newly
founded synagogues might arouse anti-Jewish passions, since formally
Islam prohibited the dhimmi from establishing new houses of worship
(Monsoniego 11). Also, the sages were concerned that synagogue activities be conducted with proper decorum, and this was more likely
where laymen had little say in their management. Rabbinic Judaism
generally has a preference for gatherings that encompass the whole of
the local population as against partial gatherings. Small groupings are
not considered very dignified, and they are considered apt to be led by
unqualified people (R. Berdugo 1891, pt. 2, 125).

The repugnance of the sages for private synagogues is particularly
expressed a statement in which Rabbi Refael Berdugo, a prominent
Meknes judge, actually goes so far as to reject the ruling of a major
fourteenth-century Spanish predecessor, Rabbi Yishaq bar-Sheishet
Perfet (Rivash). Berdugo cites Perfet as approving of the establishment
of new synagogues, but he goes on to challenge that opinion, arguing
that Perfet's position is not tenable under contemporary conditions, for
"in our times it seems to be the contrary, because several bad things
(qilqulim) come from the proliferation of synagogues" (R. Berdugo
1891, pt. 2, 125).

The sages were so bitter about the phenomenon of private synagogues that one who had failed in a case against a particular private
synagogue called upon people not to attend prayers there. Another
said that when he sent emissaries to collect for charities he refrained
from soliciting contributions in private synagogues. Whenever he
chanced to walk past such synagogues at prayer time and happened to
overhear sounds of prayer requiring responses such as "Amen," he
would ignore them. All these are elements of excommunication (Monsoniego 5; also Ovadia 11, 204; P. Berdugo, Hoshen mishpat 186).[12]
A Tetuan sage notes wistfully about a community, which he reports as
having only community synagogues and no private ones:

> The people of Gibraltar are more fortunate than we [and] all [the
> other] people of the Maghreb. For all the synagogues of the

Maghreb are of individuals . . . there is not even one that belongs
to the public. (Ben-Malka 106 end)

In the context of exerting themselves to defend the rights of established synagogues and of their rightful inheritors, the sages sought to
limit the mobility of individual congregants. The sages were apprehensive of people opening new synagogues and attracting congregants
away from the old synagogues, thus harming the latter. They, therefore, sought to discourage the shifting of congregants from one synagogue to the next. This was even felt by Ibn-Sur personally. This sage
had left his hometown Fez together with other local people, because
of political disturbance and lived for a time in Tetuan. While there,
Ibn-Sur opened a synagogue, despite the opposition of the local dignitaries. The enterprise was tolerated only when Ibn-Sur undertook to
minister to Fez refugees solely, and not to accept any veteran Tetuan
residents into his synagogue (Ben-Walid: 15b). There are community
regulations in Meknes that restrict movements between synagogues in
general:

> If an individual moves from one synagogue to the next because of
> strife, no synagogue should ever accept him [and permit him] to
> read from the Torah. One should try and induce him to go back
> to his place. (Yoseif Berdugo II: 195)

The formulation is from 1797, and it is repeated in the late nineteenth
century. But the terms of the ruling are moderate and suggest that the
legislators were aware that it would be difficult to carry this out in
practice.[13]

Frequently there arose situations where a private synagogue had already been established without permission, and closing down such a
synagogue was impossible. The opponents were reduced then to try to
establish their domination over it. We have some details of such a case
in Sefrou at the end of the eighteenth century. The community leaders
demanded to purchase half of the new synagogue from the founder,
but they lacked the necessary funds. The protagonists then agreed that
the moneys for the purchase would come from future income that the
synagogue would obtain from its congregants (Ovadia 133). The practical effect of this arrangement was to leave the new synagogue in the
hands of its lay founder.

In the eighteenth-century judgments, the sages usually continued
to favor the established synagogues over new synagogues. But in
marked contrast to the late seventeenth-century case that we saw ear-

lier, the atmosphere in the eighteenth century changed. This is well exemplified by the following Meknes case which concerned the sage of a community synagogue who had inherited his position. There functioned in that synagogue also another sage, who acted as the children's teacher. He tutored the children for payment, but had no income from the synagogue funds. Part of the congregation, the parents of the children, desiring to relieve themselves of some of the burden of tuition fees, attempted to earmark a portion of the income of the established sage for the teacher. From a strictly legal aspect, the attempt had no basis. The judge, however, ruled in favor of the teacher. He considered that there was a realistic possibility that the group of parents might secede from the synagogue, establish a new synagogue, and set the teacher up with his own serara. Such an eventuality would both have cost the established sage diminution in the income of his synagogue and have led to the establishment of a new synagogue. Since the judge considered that material injury to the established sage was imminent either way, he ruled so as to avoid an additional undesirable outcome (R. Berdugo 1891, pt. 2, 140).[14] Such incidents are the background to the apprehensions and feelings of insecurity of established sages about their positions, despite the legality of their positions (Ovadia 117, 127).

During the course of the eighteenth century, the position of the mellah sages on the issue of private synagogues thus underwent a change. While at the outset it was unambiguously inimical, in time it became more permissive. In the writings of a late nineteenth-century sage, there is a remarkable reference to the eighteenth-century Fez judge, Sarfati, referred to in an earlier chapter. Sarfati is mentioned as having been an opponent of new synagogues. Late in his career Sarfati changed his position and permitted the foundation of new synagogues. Sarfati is quoted expounding on the reasoning underlying his varying judgments. On a particular precedent he found, Sarfati remarks revealingly:

> It is true indeed that I was not cognizant of this ruling . . . and now that I have once more delved into the sources and seen the aforementioned ruling I am overjoyed. For in the past, when I used to write judgments on this subject that were contrary to the present one, I had pangs of conscience (*libi noqfi*). (R. M. Elbaz, Yoreh dei'a 1)

We are thus made privy to the feelings of this judge and the sentiments underlying his change of judgment.

The change in the attitude of the sages toward private synagogues developed further in the nineteenth century. The sages became tolerant toward, and increasingly accepted the existence of, private synagogues. We encounter new considerations that the judges bring to bear upon their judgments in favor of private synagogues. One is that the consideration of monetary loss for the sages in established synagogues is not weighty enough to preclude the opening of new ones (Ya'aqov Berdugo, Hoshen mishpat 31). Another consideration is that prohibition to open a private synagogue might lead to strife (A. Anqawe 6). In another judgment, the old prohibition becomes delimited in a novel way. It is made to apply to laymen only, but sages are permitted to establish their own synagogues. This innovation attains a rudimentary theoretical formulation in an early nineteenth-century Fez ruling concerning the insistence of the Sefrou sage Abitbul to open his own synagogue. At first the court ruled against him, basing itself on the old prohibitions. Later the court reversed judgment on the grounds that the plaintiff was a sage. "For why," the court argued, "should he be entitled to less than the other sages?" (Ovadia 133).

We encounter a further innovative step toward the acceptance of private synagogues in the course of the career of the Rabbi Refael Moshe Elbaz of Sefrou. In one of his first judgments, in 1854, this sage ruled according to the negative precedents, presenting the traditional arguments (the material rights of the established sages and apprehension for synagogue decorum). In a ruling at the end of his career forty years later, however, Elbaz deliberately changed his position. He limited the prohibition to laymen only, and elaborated that the considerations that had moved the legislators and judges of the past applied no more. He challenged the notion that the founders of new synagogues act out of haughty and political considerations and seek to dominate others. On the contrary, Elbaz argued, the founders of synagogues offer a public service as people require more synagogue facilities. For currently, Elbaz states, the synagogues are all filled to capacity, and they also serve as school premises for children (R. M. Elbaz, Orah hayim 8).

As the nineteenth century proceeded, the sages increasingly faced the problem of formulating a general policy concerning private synagogues. The solution they arrived at was that the founder would transfer the synagogue to the community formally, as a legal fiction, similar to the resolution of the Sefrou case noted above. The community would then place the facility at the disposal of the individual, as "a pawn" (*mashkon*), and he would manage it at his discretion. This

procedure was aimed at maintaining some sort of compatibility between the traditional preference for community synagogues and the
new reality of proliferating private synagogues (Ovadia 205; Yoseif
Berdugo II: 194). In substance, however, little was left of the old
preference for community synagogues.

Having outlined the historical course of synagogue organization
during the eighteenth and nineteenth centuries, I turn to its salient
sociological features. The mellah people invested emotions and energy
in arguments about synagogues "of the community" and "of individuals," and to them the differences were very important. From a sociological perspective, however, the commonalty of all synagogues of
mellah times is more salient than the differences. Even the community
synagogues were, for most practical purposes, managed as if they were
private property, since the sages who operated in them were based
upon hereditary rights (serara). These rights extended the authority of
the officiating sages, both at the expense of the wider communal, ex-
trasynagogue authorities, and at the expense of the individuals who
composed the synagogue congregation internally. Thus Ibn-Sur ruled:

> The leaders of the city do not have the right to impose their
> authority on the community of a synagogue, that does not belong
> to them, and in which they do not pray. They may not decree to
> appoint another prayer-leader . . . for that does not concern
> [them]. (Ibn-Sur, vol. 2, 177)

Just as "the leaders of the city" were limited in their power, so also
were the synagogue congregants, as emerges from the following late
eighteenth-century statement:

> We see [that any] high-handed person (ish zeroa) [who so desires],
> builds a synagogue for himself, and installs there anyone whom
> he pleases, to officiate. And the community cannot complain . . .
> And further we see, that when a prayer-leader does not want an
> individual of the congregation to pray at his synagogue—he ex-
> pels him (doheihu), (Elkhreif: 13)

Remarkably, the statement refers in the same context to two different
types of synagogue managers, haughty laymen and regular sages. But
their style of management is reportedly the same.

In the context of the wider mellah society, the synagogues thus had
considerable autonomy. Within the synagogues the focus of power lay
with the synagogue managers and not with the congregants. The synagogues were conceived of as private property, largely so in the case

of community synagogues, and totally so in the case of synagogues founded by individuals.[15] Hence we encounter business transactions in which synagogues figure as capital. They had a market value, could be sold and bought, and presented as collateral for debts (Monsoniego 6; Ovadia 504; R. Berdugo 1891, 341; and many others).

Because of their material value, synagogues figure frequently in litigations, particularly in inheritance cases involving sages with rival claims to the right to officiate and enjoy synagogue incomes. The concern of judges was to distinguish rightful inheritors from other claimants, and they acted very forthrightly to ensure that inheritance proceeds lawfully. One such case involved the widow of a sage who, in her need, had sold the inheritance right (*serara*) of her husband, in disregard of the deceased sage's son. The court declared the sale void, despite complicated ramifications that this decision aroused (R. Berdugo 1891, 286). In another judgment a sage was so zealous for the lawful rights of an inheritor that he supported the claim of one despite his having moved away from the locality, thus being unable to officiate (R. Berdugo 1891, 155). In yet another case, an inheritor obtained the support of a court despite the fact that for the past two generations sages of other families had officiated in the contended synagogue (Ben-Malka 24). Even when an inheritor was not qualified to act as prayer leader, the sages extended support to him. The solution for such an inheritor was to hire a sage to officiate in the synagogue, pay him a salary, and share with him the income of the synagogue gained from the congregants (Yoseif Berdugo I, 1974: 101–102). Strikingly, the sages supported synagogue claimants, even in cases based on matrilineal kinship (Elmaleh 3; Yoseif Berdugo I, 1974: 89; Elkhreif 9).

As against the numerous instances of the courts supporting inheritance claims, there are only a few cases where the sages overruled such claims. An instance of that kind occurred in a Meknes case involving a plaintiff who had been a minor when he lost his father, who had been a prayer leader. During the plaintiff's minority the congregation had appointed another sage as acting prayer leader, but now the court upheld the plea of the latter to retain the position (P. Berdugo, Hoshen mishpat 187). Also another Meknes case, that we discussed earlier, where a judge apprehensive of a synagogue split ruled against an inheritor, should be seen in this context.

The virtually consistent support that the sages offered those who inherited synagogue positions led them frequently to face problems posed by rightful inheritors who, however, were not personally qualified to act as synagogue leaders. In cases of "community synagogues," the sages ruled that the pertinent rights reverted to the community (Elkhreif 9; Moshe Berdugo 9; Yoseif Berdugo I, 1974: 101–102; also Elmaleh, vol. 2, 56; Quriat 61). This limitation of the right of inheritance is based by one authority, on the consideration that "the holiness [of community synagogues] is profound" (Yoseif Berdugo I, 1974: 101–102). In contrast to that, the landed property of private synagogues belongs to individuals. Therefore, even if an inheritor is unqualified to officiate, he remains the owner of the premises. When such a synagogue is activated, with the cooperation of a hired qualified sage, the owner is entitled to a portion of the income (Quriat 61; Elmaleh, vol. 2, 56).

The determination of the portion to which, under these circumstances, the inheritor is entitled differs according to local custom. That of Marrakesh and southern Morocco was that a lay inheritor, unqualified to officiate, could hire a sage and install him in the synagogue to act in his stead. The layman, after payment of the sage's salary, was entitled to all the income of the synagogue. According to the custom of Fez and the rest of Morocco, the sage who was installed in a synagogue under the aforementioned circumstances was entitled to all the income, and he had to pay the lay owner only rental for the premises (Elmaleh, vol. 2, 56). The rationale underlying this position is, that

> [monetary] vows and gifts [to synagogues] are made in honor of the Torah. Whoever has Torah honor may partake from it, but not he who has not (*mi she'yeshno bi'khvod ha'torah yitol bi'khvoda, velo mi she'eino bi'khvod ha'torah*). (Yoseif Berdugo, I, 1974: 101–102; also Quriat 61)

This sentiment of the sages was formulated as a regulation (which we have on hand in the writings of Meknes sages of the Berdugo family in the nineteenth century, and the legislation is attributed to the eighteenth century):

> Even if some unlettered person (*eize hamoni*) obtains a synagogue by purchase, it is the duty of the judges who oversee (*beit-din hamashgihim*) the rule of order, to depose him from his governance. He should receive rental for the premises and no more. The rest should be given for maintenance of the facility or for sages who study Torah. (Ya'aqov Berdugo, Yore dei'a 6; Yoseif Berdugo II: 163)

This difference between the practices of the Marrakesh and Fez regions is sociologically significant. According to the former, the scope of the potency of the lay individual is enhanced. When such a person acquires or inherits a synagogue, he governs its income and only pays a salary to the officiating sage. According to the practice of Fez, the domain of the layman is delimited. He may not benefit from moneys given in "honor of the Torah"; those accrue to the officiating sage. The rights of the layman are circumscribed, and the sage must pay him rental only.

The difference of custom of the regions of Marrakesh and Fez is linked to a general problem of Moroccan-Jewish society outlined in Chapter 1, that of the relations between the Sephardic and the indigenous Jews. This dates back to late medieval times when the Sephardic refugees from Spain succeeded in dominating northern and central Morocco, whereas in the south of the country the indigenous Jews continued to predominate. In several areas of social and religious life there were differences between those who retained the indigenous traditions and those who carried the Sephardic traditions. In religious life, there was some squabbling over practices of ritual slaughtering until about 1530. There were also social differences that led the two populations to maintain separate synagogues and cemeteries over the centuries (Bentov 1986). In the area of family life also we shall, in Chapter 8, observe another difference. On the whole, the indigenous tradition of Morocco weakened in time, and the hegemony of the Sephardim and their culture became established. It is significant, however, that in certain areas of life indigenous practices not only remained vital but were even adopted by the erstwhile carriers of the Sephardic tradition. Such is the case with the difference of customs in respect to laymen managing private synagogues: in the nineteenth century the Marrakesh custom became accepted in the Fez and Meknes heartland of the Sephardic tradition. We turn now to the details of that process.

From the statement of a nineteenth-century Meknes sage we learn that by his time the old Sephardic practice of central Morocco had been definitely abrogated:

> The first rabbis of Fez and Meknes (may the memory of the pious ones in paradise be a blessing) ruled [as follows]: A person who left a synagogue to his sons, some of whom are qualifed to fill his place and some of whom are not—the qualified ones only may receive [the income of] vows and gifts [to the synagogue] . . . However, such is not our custom: Even the unqualified may re-

ceive [income] from the heritage (*serara*) of the synagogue . . .
for after all he can hire a prayer-leader [to officiate] in his stead.
(Yoseif Berdugo I, 1974: 101–102)

Even laymen are thus entitled to authority in private synagogues in
Meknes, if specific professional religious services are obtained through
hiring—all according to the Marrakesh custom. This stands in contrast to the ruling of the "first rabbis of Fez and Meknes," who were
stricter and more sensitive about the rights of sages. The implication
of the change is the diffusion of a custom, which emphasizes and mag-
nifies the role of the individual who inherits, although he cannot officiate as a sage. Another ramification of this is to elevate the status of
the successful and outstanding individual who acquires or builds a
synagogue while lacking in rabbinical attributes. This is a further
stage of the development that we saw embryonically in the eighteenth
century, when the sages exhibited an attitude toward private synagogues, albeit inimical but more relaxed than that of their seventeenth-century predecessors.

The nineteenth-century sages were evidently aware that they were
governing their communities differently than had been done in the
past. Besides the foregoing statement, we have the remarkable revela-
tion of a Fez judge, who brings to bear in his argumentation a precedent by a major Sephardic authority, the thirteenth-century Rabbi
Shlomo ben-Adrat (Rashba). Ben-Adrat had ruled that under certain
circumstances a sage could be dismissed from his position. The Fez
sage dismisses this weighty precedent:

> Nevertheless I hesitate (*hokeikh*) in the matter, for perhaps that
> [judgment of Ben-Adrat applied] only in the time of Rabbi
> Shlomo ben-Adrat (may his merit protect us, Amen) . . . but in
> our time any prayer-leader who is dismissed . . . becomes pub-
> licly suspect . . . that there is in him something defiled (*sad
> pesul*), far be it from us. (Monsoniego 10)

The latter-day judge is thus moved by a certain specific social concern
(which unfortunately he does not reveal),[16] to reject the pertinent ruling of a very important predecessor. The Fez decision reflects a situation where greater power is attributed to the prominent individual (in
this case the incumbent synagogue sage) than in the past. The judgment also reflects a conscious distancing from the Sephardic tradition.
The principle of synagogue inheritance (serara) is thus extended and
made to apply more widely than in the past.

The sages of the nineteenth century did not arrive at this position easily. In the eighteenth century we found them wavering between their principled favor for community synagogues managed by hereditary sages, and the felt social pressures of ambitious individuals, who aimed to have their own hereditary synagogues. One insightful eighteenth-century judge, Rabbi Ya'aqov Toledano of Meknes, noticed the incipient development in the judgments of his colleagues. Referring to the tendency to extend the concept of serara beyond the precedents of the Sephardic sages, Toledano writes caustically:

> I have seen several court rulings (*pisqey dinim*) of all sorts (*minim miminim shonim*), that totally lack foundation in the Talmud. They are [based on] mere allusion (*asmakhta be'alma*) to [a] biblical verse. ". . .the annointed priest . . . from among his sons" (Lev. 6.15). And all that is worthless to me; and I do not agree—to come up with a new Torah, out of speculation (*sevarat ha'rosh*) and biblical allusions . . . !? (Moshe Berdugo: 66)

Toledano is keenly aware of the weak legal basis of some of the new judgments on synagogue matters of the sages of his times.

This leads us to the question as to why the history of mellah synagogues should run this course. What are the sociocultural forces that cause the emergence of new synagogues and of individuals who aggrandize themselves? The people of the mellah themselves explained the change that overcame their synagogue policy. Rabbi Moshe Toledano of Meknes recounts the appearance in print of the responsa collection of the Duran family sages (*Seifer tashbeis,* the great tome that had lain in manuscript in Algiers for hundreds of years). He links this publication event with the time when the Meknes sages still held that unqualified lay inheritors of private synagogues were entitled to rental only. In the to him previously unknown Seifer tashbeis, Toledano found a ruling that legitimatized, in his opinion, the expanded right of inheritance, contrary to the then prevailing practice. Thereupon, Toledano recounts, he changed that practice and began to rule according to the Marrakesh practice which accorded the Duran rulings (M. Toledano: 57).

This account, I suggest, provides an insight into the rationalization process that permitted a contemporary sage to change his mind. But, clearly, one would require also a knowledge of the motives that led the sage to desire this change. Without such a desire, the source in the newly published manuscript that came to his attention would not have fired his imagination. An approach to the problem is suggested by the comments of David Ovadia (1975–1985, vol 3: 112–114) that there was a significant expansion of population in the communities in the nineteenth century, and the existing public facilities became insufficient. Also, the nature of the community organization that we uncovered in the foregoing chapters was such that the communities could not cope very well with the new situation. I suggest that these conditions offered scope for the initiative of individuals, and at the same time weakened the resistance of the guardians of the ancient communal traditions.

We do not, at this stage of our understanding of mellah society, have a full solution to the problem. It is notable, however, that the course of mellah synagogue development dovetails general developments of Moroccan society and culture (outlined above in Chap. 2). The essential feature of those developments is the continued growth of informal charismatic social forces—religious and political—at the expense of the formally institutionalized elements (for instance, the rising marabout authority as against that of the ulama). Among the Jews these processes developed at a slower pace, for the dominance of halakha sages was marked, both in the great communities of Fez and Meknes as well in small ones deep in the Atlas Mountains hinterland. Within that context, however, the stamp of the society and culture in which they lived made its mark also on the Jews of Morocco.

We come finally to the social ramifications of the mellah synagogue sociology that we have uncovered. The mellah people invested much energy in disputes about the establishment, inheritance, and management of synagogues. Evidently, they attributed great importance to the issues that we have been discussing. One must expect, then, that the issues that so concerned the mellah people had profound ramifications in their lives. One such ramification is the powerful individualistic and spontaneous element in mellah self-rule, which is consistent with and dovetails the type of increasingly popular synagogue organization that we have uncovered. Another ramification is linked to the point on which I dwelt at the beginning of this chapter, namely, that the mellah synagogues did not fill as many functions as they might, in areas such as learning and education. We encountered indications of many activities taking place in private homes. Considering the great investment, material and emotional, of people in their synagogues, this is astonishing and warrants some attention.

I suggest that this feature of mellah social life be considered jointly with the prevalence of the individual and private element in Moroccan synagogue life. People who had the means had their own synagogues in which most of the congregants were, as we have seen, virtually guests. Given the particular Middle Eastern relationship of host and guest, which implies marked inferiority of the latter, one may assume that many people yearned for an arena where they could express their religiosity and culture in a more self-enhancing way. Hence, the practice of engaging in religious matters precisely away from the synagogues and from their domineering masters, both sage and lay. Even individuals who did not themselves host a Zohar-reading circle in their own homes might prefer occasionally, when expressing their religiosity, to frequent the home of a peer and not to be constantly subject to the master of their synagogue.

The great salience of the synagogues in the politics, religion, and culture of the mellah affords a vivid insight into the interplay between individual and community in social life. In the next chapter, we depart from the arena of public life and delve into the private domain of the family, to examine there again that central problematic of Moroccan Jewish society, the tension between the individual and the community.

8 FAMILY LIFE: INDIVIDUALS AMONG THEIR RELATIVES

The fundamental element of the family life of the mellah people was its extension beyond the confines of "the nuclear family." While the ties that bound the married couple and their off-spring were very meaningful, this narrow family circle was bound intricately within a net of more distant relatives, to form an extended family. The nuclear family had an identity of its own and a measure of self-sufficiency, yet it was part of, and enmeshed in, a wider family unit. The ensuing tension between independence and integration of the individual within family relationships was a common concern of the people of the mellah. Throughout our study of Moroccan Jewish institutions, we have seen how commonly people were conceived of in terms of the specific social contexts in which they interacted, and not only in terms of ascribed social attributes. The study of family life in the mellah presents an opportunity to clarify the nature of the group that constitutes a family, to examine the nature of the boundaries that enclose the family, and the hold of the family group over its individual members of various ages and both sexes.

The Moroccan Jewish nuclear family was not clearly distinct from other branches of the extended family, and its independence both as an economic and as a domestic unit was usually limited. Adult sons often shared business and home with fathers and brothers and participated in patriarchal arrangements. Typically, men blessed each other that they should be "surrounded with sons" (Ovadia 649). Patriarchal domestic arrangements entailed adult sons living with their spouses and children in proximity to their father and married brothers. They all resided in compounds that centered on a common courtyard, and each nuclear family had private rooms. This was the preferred way of living in which the blessing was manifest. A late nineteenth-century Alliance Israélite Universelle report (cited in Chouraqui 1952: 223–224) permits us an insight into the size of the mellah family. The Jewish community of Meknes was reported, according to this source, to number about 6,000 individuals composing 1,137 families.[1] Thus, the average number of persons per family was a little under 5.3. After allowance is made for some child mortality, and the number of parents in the family is deducted, we arrive at an average of three children per family. Assuming the number of sons and daughters to be equal, the average number of married sons constituting an extended household together with their parents was thus no more than 1.5. This figure, given the high incidence of infant mortality in eighteenth- and nineteenth-century Morocco, should not be considered low. On the contrary, I view the figure as tending to overrate the size of the family during most of our period, because the data derive from the last years of the nineteenth century, a time when the population had begun to expand (see Chap. 3).

During the course of the nineteenth century, the population density in the mellahs increased, due to natural fertility and to migration from tribal areas. Consequently, patrilocality became increasingly common. In addition to the basic ideology that favored patrilocality, a new material factor emerged that enhanced the trend. As numerous European travelers in Morocco remarked, the urban Jewish quarters became increasingly congested in the nineteenth century.[2] Therefore, even when heads of related nuclear families were inclined to separate their households, they were often unable to do so, due to sheer lack of available dwellings. A late nineteenth-century Meknes sage refers to the living conditions of a married couple who, living patrilocally, did not have their own room but only part of a room separated by a drape. This sage states, generally, that many fathers of married sons insisted that their offspring live with them patrilocally under such conditions, because of their dire poverty (H. Meshash: 224). There are further indications of such conditions in nineteenth-century reports of cases of promiscuity, linked to crowded living conditions and lack of privacy, and the attempts of rabbis to prohibit married couples from living in very close proximity to other people (Ya'aqov Berdugo, Even ha'ezer 84; see also the later R. Anqawe 1930, 14). However, judging from numerous reports by contemporary European visitors who were struck by the crowded conditions of the Jewish quarters, these attempts were probably not very effective.

Patriarchal and patrilocal living caused particular hardship for the bride, who came to live with the family of the groom. Brides were young, only a few years beyond maturity and sometimes younger than that, and they suffered from the natural difficulties involved in the abrupt move from their parental home without any significant preparation or period of adjustment. As a young wife, the bride was subjected to the dominance of both her husband and his parents. The adjustment was facilitated by the fact that frequently there had been extensive social contact between the families of the bride and of the groom before marriage. After marriage, neighborly contact enabled the young bride to make frequent visits to her parents, in particular to her mother. The parental support gained through this contact eased the adjustment problems of the bride in her new situation. On the other hand, distance from a bride's parental home was a source of distress. A recurrent theme in disputes between spouses, as presented before the sages, were the adamant objections of women to the requests of husbands to move to other localities, away from their hometowns. However, husbands often insisted on moving, because of the economic and business pressures to which they were more sensitive than their secluded wives (Ovadia 440; also the later R. Anqawe 1910, 9). We even hear of couples who lived in separation, because the wives refused to follow their husbands who had been driven by economic circumstances to distant places (Ibn-Sur 69; see also A. Anqawe, Hoshen mishpat 130).

On the whole, attachment to the hometown on the part of men and women was strong, as we saw in another context (Chap. 3). This attachment was particularly strong with women who, not being involved in the pursuit of a livelihood, were not very aware of the relative economic merits of various localities. We find among married women concerted efforts to prevent husbands from moving. Particularly during the first years of marriage, the welfare of a woman depended to a considerable extent on the moral and sentimental support that she drew from her natal kin.

We have an early twentieth-century letter sent from Meknes to the head of the court in Tangier, which tells of a disputing Tangier couple who had moved there from their hometown of Meknes. The writer had produced the letter on behalf of his neighbor, the mother of the Tangier woman. The mother appealed from distant Meknes to the Tangier sage to succor her daughter, whose husband was reported (in an earlier letter from the daughter to her mother)

to oppress and torment her greatly. He beats and curses her. In
his rage he smashes and tears apart all the household belongings.
She has no peace with him. (Y. Meshash 1970: 141)

Evidently, the Meknes woman, in despair about the situation of her
daughter, was unable to resolve the situation by merely relying on
local Tangier people, relatives and neighbors, to intervene informally.
She and her daughter felt they had to involve the authorities through
a complicated long-distance correspondence. On the other hand, spatial proximity between the families of the groom and the bride helped
the bride adjust to the patrilocal family. Also old-established social ties
between the families were helpful. In the absence of such ties, particularly when the families of the groom and of the bride lived in distant
communities, prejudice leading to friction between the bride and her
in-laws was apt to become potent. This is well expressed in the letter
of a Sefrou woman, on the subject of a match for her son, that we saw
in Chapter 3.

In cases of marital ties between spatially distant families, the bride
could not expect much effective support from her natal kin. It seems,
therefore, that there was a widespread tendency for marriages to be
contracted between local people, with neighbors or kinsmen arranging
matches between their children. This contention is supported by the
fact that the role of the matchmaker (*shadkhan*), so well entrenched
in traditional European Jewry, was unknown in Morocco. Indeed, in
marriages that were predominantly local, between families who had
rubbed shoulders in one community for many generations and who
were possibly already related, the services of a formal middleman were
not needed. Among Ashkenazic Jews, on the other hand, the role of
the matchmaker was linked to an educational system that led many
young men to move away from their hometowns. Marital links were
thus frequently established between distant communities, the teachers
sometimes serving as matchmakers. Among Moroccan Jews there was
no comparable mobility, because of the quite different educational system in which learning beyond the elementary level was embedded in
particular rabbinical families, as we saw in Chapter 7.[3] The dual link-
age of learning, to family and to locality, precluded any significant
movement of marriageable students away from their hometowns. Marriages arranged by parents were accepted by the young as a matter of
course. In one court case, the issue was the claim of a bride's father

against the father of the groom for damage payment, because the young man had broken an engagement arranged by the parents. Against this the defendant pleaded that this was "an exceptional accident, because all sons agree to the choice of their fathers" (Abitbul, vol. 2, 4). The defendant argued, in effect, that repudiation by young people of an arrangement agreed upon by the parents constitutes *force majeure,* and that one is not to be held responsible for such an extraordinary eventuality. The argument reveals the sentiments of the times.[4]

The patrilocal arrangement, whereby the bride came to live with the groom's family, was problematic not only for the bride but also for the groom, and in particular, for the groom's mother. In the aforementioned letter by the Sefrou woman concerning the selection of a bride, the mother advises against choosing a very young bride, for "I cannot raise a little girl" (Ovadia 401). Child marriage added to the responsibility of the mother-in-law, who now would have to see to the needs of her very young daughter-in-law besides those of her own children. An agreement arrived at between a disputing couple, which has come down to us, reflects some of the problems that stemmed from the frivolity of a very young bride. According to this document, the bride was categorically ordered to obey her mother-in-law. Also, she was ordered

> not to give away any of the belongings of her husband, to neither relative nor stranger, except with the permission of her husband or of his mother. (Ovadia 581; also Ibn-Sur 181)

The proximity of a married woman's natal home permitted maintaining ties and provided support, but proximity could also cause strife. The interference of the bride's natal family in the affairs of the bride and her husband, and in her relations with her in-laws, could disrupt harmony.

In another case of a disputing couple, we find the bride's father a party to a formal agreement reached between the couple. According to this, he committed himself to restrain his wife (the bride's mother) from causing strife in her daughter's home (Ovadia 400). In general, very strong ties between a woman and her natal family were frowned upon, because such ties were considered as potentially leading to discord. Writing about a married woman in another case of marital strife, a sage summarized the situation as follows:

She does not spend time at home. Most of the day she is in her father's house. And as a result she does not do household chores for her husband. (Ovadia 347)

The fathers of grooms were apprehensive of such situations. Therefore, we find marriage contracts that have clauses regulating the ties between the bride and her natal family. The contracts seek to limit the frequency of a bride's visit to her parents. In one such document, the bride is ordered "not to go to her father's house more than once a week" (Ovadia 645). This particular contract preceded marriage, and it is phrased abstractly, before the young people actually experienced married life. It expresses the desired norm of relationships and visiting patterns, namely, that it is fine and accepted for a married daughter to visit her parents once a week, no more and no less.[5]

That, however, does not reflect reality. For the latter, we must turn to agreements made by disputing couples who already lived together, were a little older and more experienced. In one such case, the sage rules on the question of visiting frequency:

The wife should not leave her home often, even in order to go to her father's house. She may go there only two or three times weekly, for work that she does together with her mother. (Ovadia 374)

The husband's relatives seek here, through the ruling of the sage, to control the ties between the wife and her natal family. Control pertains both to the frequency and to the content of the visits. Visits that have concrete content, such as engaging in housework or handicraft, are permitted. But socializing per se is discouraged. We hear of a case, albeit early in the twentieth century, of a husband who ordered his wife under oath not to leave the house more than once or twice a month, and even then only after having received his written permission (R. Anqawe 1930, 86). It is difficult to imagine that this was carried out in practice, but the case demonstrates the fundamental sentiment of the times concerning proper domestic behavior.[6] In the court decision involving this particular couple, the judge ruled more realistically,

And at times when her husband is out of town, and she will have to visit the sick, or her mother, or go to the house of the bereaved, or to a house of celebration—she may do so. (R. Anqawe 1930, 86)

The mores for enclosing women in the domestic setting are powerfully reflected in the pronouncement of a sage on verbal agressions. Anyone who calls a woman "a whore" is to be whipped, ruled the sage. However, the offender is not liable, if he claims that he did not mean to say the woman was actually promiscuous but only that she wanders out of her house frequently (Yoseif Berdugo I, 1922–1943: 41b).

Socializing among women is thus delimited to certain situations, the common element of which is that they are linked with traditional pious deeds (misvot).[7] The misvot of women focus on the domestic setting, not the public synagogue setting. We hear very little of women attending synagogue services. Often the mellah houses of prayer did not have a separate gallery or aisle for women (in Sefrou, reports Ovadia 1975–1985, vol. 3: 114, there was none until the late nineteenth century). But even where such an aisle was available it was not used much.[8] The extreme sensitivity to female menstrual impurity permitted only women in menopause to relax and attend religious services regularly. Younger women were subject to the domination of the older women and were secluded in their homes.

In contrast to the problematic nature of the ties of married women with their natal families, the ties of both women and their husbands with the relatives of the latter were straightforward. In the context of patrilocal families, those ties were of such paramount importance, and so routinely accepted, that they are seldom mentioned in marriage contracts and figure but rarely in disputes and jurisdiction. Since people usually resided patrilocally, visiting the husband's parents was not an issue. Occasionally people lived matrilocally, but that was exceptional.[9]

Besides being detached to a considerable extent from their families of origin, and subordinate to the kin of the husband, married women had little say in economic activities. They were excluded from the affairs of men and also did not run independent economic ventures of their own. We see the latter only in connection with widowed or deserted women. Women being altogether confined thus commanded few resources in the domestic arena. They were not part of the dyadic complex of patron-client relationships that was pervasive in the culture of Morocco. The sociopolitical position of women was consequently humble. This is trenchantly expressed in the aforementioned discourse on verbal abuse and on the punishments to be meted out for various verbal offenses. The sage footnotes his discussion saying that all the rules he explicated apply to offending males only. However, "as to women: since it is their custom to utter curses and imprecations, nonsense and falsehood—their words are immaterial" (Yoseif Berdugo I, 1922–1943: 41b). Women are then beneath punishment for offenses on a person's honor. Consequently, they cannot fill an overt role in a political system that hinges to a great extent on male conceptions of honor and dishonor.

Also in disputes between a married woman and her mother-in-law and other powerful domestic personages, the position of the former was weak. The intervention of such a woman's brothers and parents in her favor, in cases of domestic conflict in a patrilocale, could theoretically have been of consequence. Our sources, however, do not reflect many such activities. In only one case of domestic conflict do the woman's relatives appear in the role of protectors, and even then ineffectively. The case involved a man who desired to take a second wife against the objection of his spouse, but he was apprehensive of the violent reaction of his brothers-in-law, and therefore contracted the marriage in secret (Ibn-Sur 288). The dearth of specific cases in which women were protected by agnates, coupled with the numerous cases of domestic conflict in general that have reached us, lead to an important conclusion. Namely, that conflict between spouses was generally contained in domestic privacy and did not often spill over into the public domain. Under these conditions, the major power resource available to women lay in the area of uxorial rights that concerned the husband and wife individually, the area of sexual relations and domestic services.

Household chores included primarily the preparation of food and the treatment of clothing. If one can extrapolate from the division of labor that was current among recently arrived traditional Moroccan immigrants in Israel, to the situation of the past, it would seem that the domain of food preparation was not an exclusively female preserve. Men played an important role in it, because the preparation of meat, a major item of nutrition, required particular ritual skills. Certain sinews and layers of fat are halakhically prohibited, and had to be removed. Also, the blood had to be drained completely. The execution of these tasks, while not relegated to professionals as they are in certain other Jewish societies, were considered important and performed by adult males only (Shokeid 1971: 166). And of course the purchasing of food for the household was a male task, because the market, as in the Muslim world in general, was primarily a male arena. The handling of clothes, in contrast to that, was a female activity, and the participation of men was restricted to purchasing the material in the market. Men did not engage in needlework at home, despite the fact that many made their living from crafts associated with the garment trade, such as tailors and button makers.[10] In case of domestic strife, women were in a position to withhold certain crucial personal services from their husbands. They could disrupt routine treatment of clothing, and to a considerable extent also the daily preparation of food.

The major female potential in domestic strife, however, lay in the area of conjugal relations. Sexual relations between husband and wife throughout traditional Jewry are governed by norms of "family purity." These entail a cycle of separation and reunion dependent on the menses, and prior to reunion wives are required to immerse in a ritualarium (*miqve*). The correct time for immersion requires constant attention to the calendar and self-examination as to the personal condition. In Moroccan Jewry, these matters were virtually governed by womenfolk: the wives themselves and to a considerable extent their elder kinswomen. But the norms of family purity naturally also concerned husbands. Theoretically, maintenance of these norms could have been supervised by men, as were many other areas of life. Yet this was not the case.

In other times and places of the Jewish Diaspora, the norms of family purity were governed by females to a lesser extent, and male rabbis had a say. In Eastern Europe, for instance, problems of family purity were frequently brought to the attention of rabbis by the husbands. Two categories of males were thus involved. In southern Tunisia we actually hear of a specific rabbinical appointment to rule over such problems (Deshen 1982). And in contemporary Israel, the popular religious literature includes manuals for grooms, booklets to assist them with the calendrical calculations. In Moroccan mellah society, the regulation of married female sexuality seems to have been in the hands of women to a relatively greater extent. Only the more unusual cases of physiological disorders appear in the records as having been brought to the attention of the sages. In the intimacy of domestic life, routine female decision as to proper immersion times, afforded women an outlet for self-assertion and power.

Sexuality was thus a resource that enabled women to disrupt or to permit conjugal relations. The following summary of a plea of a husband reflects a scenario where a wife engaged in sexual politics, which often lead to divorce:

> She curses his parents in his presence. He overcomes himself and does not curse her parents because of his respect for them. But he cannot restrain himself and continue to hear her curses and therefore he struck her . . . And she does not go to immerse, or does so at improper times. (Ovadia 406, 374)

The power of women lay primarily in the intimacy of the domestic setting. Women usually lacked the force to bring domestic strife into public view. Not only the harassed Meknes woman in Tangier whom we encountered above, but also local women seemed to lack power to call upon effective allies when engaged in domestic strife.

It is important in this context to indicate a range of potential activity about which the sources are silent. We do not hear of ramified cases of domestic quarrels that drove kinsmen to take action. The brothers of married women do figure occasionally in case material in support of their sister. But they figure only marginally, and do not seem to exert themselves effectively, or to mobilize wider support on behalf of the woman.[11] In an ethnography of contemporary Israel, describing Moroccan Jewish immigrants during the early years of resettlement, we hear of quarrels spilling over into public view and kinsmen and neighbors being called upon for support (Shokeid 1982). However, the flareups, while noisy and verbose, were of short duration and did not involve broad restructuring of social alliances or a ramified set of activities involving kinsmen. The silence of our legal materials on these matters is thus consistent with ethnographic observations. This leads to the conclusion that the embedment of the mellah nuclear family within the extended family does not seem to have been very deep.

Squabbling spouses, however, did involve kinsmen in their disputes. The sources report that spouses hurled imprecations at each other, in which those relatives figured. These data, together with the silence of the sources on more ramified involvement of kinsmen in domestic disputes, need to be considered jointly, in order to depict the nature of the family in mellah society. The involvement of the nuclear family within the extended family is evident in the way people customarily try to encourage or dissuade others from taking action. People mention the ancestors of the person addressed, and suggest that complying with the request would be in keeping with respect for the memory of the dead, or would benefit the soul in paradise. Here is one example: "I beg of you . . . in the names of the righteous ones, the foundations of the universe and in the names of the souls of your holy ancestors" (Ovadia 404). Another request has a rebuke: ". . . you ought to have considered the reputation of your holy ancestors, and thought of the shame that you have brought onto the family" (Ovadia 271).

In economic activities, the interdependence of the nuclear family and the extended family was particularly evident at the time of marriage. Wedding gifts offered by kinsmen and friends were usually given to the father of the groom "in honor of the groom," not to the groom himself. This practice parallels the donations made by friends and relatives of the young married couple to the synagogue, again "in honor of the groom." Such donations are promised to the synagogue sage or to the synagogue fund on the Sabbath after the wedding, when relatives and friends are called upon individually to read from the Torah.[12] In both these kinds of donations, gift making is enmeshed in the wider community and in the extended family. Gift making bolsters the community and the family, not necessarily the new nuclear family that is being founded. As a rule, the father of the groom did not distinguish the wedding gifts from his other property. The married son often participated in the economic activities of the father, whether handicraft or business, as a junior partner and thus benefited from the family property in general (Ovadia 586).[13] The bride, on her part, built her household within that of her in-laws and under their control.

Under these conditions the married son had no great need for personal capital. The incorporation of the nuclear family within the extended patrilocal family concerned both consumption (within the domestic sphere that was governed mainly by women), and production (within the sphere of handicrafts and commerce governed by men). The bride was usually endowed by her father with a dowry of the trousseau type, comprising her personal effects, finery, and jewelry. The bride was also given gifts of clothing by the groom and his father. But, importantly, we do not hear of more economically liquid dowries, in the form of cash, given by kinsmen of the bride to the groom and his kinsmen. Dowries, thus, did not constitute assets of import in ongoing economic activities.

Also, we hear little of bridewealth beyond that of the standard Jewish *ketuba*-type. This meant, in effect, that payment of bridewealth on the part of the groom was delayed to such a time when the wife lost her husband, either through divorce or death (in which case it was paid out of the estate of the husband). In the absence of these eventualities, bridewealth was not due. But whatever the eventuality, the ketuba arrangement was of minimal import for ongoing economic activities, and also of little concern to the kinsmen of the couple. A large ketuba sum only insured the woman personally in event of a future disaster. And as far as the kinsmen of the couple were concerned, a generous ketuba merely reflected, in a general and abstract form, their opulence and status.

In certain other Jewish societies the material ramifications of marriages were more salient. Dowries, transferred from the father of the bride to the groom, were prominent in Ashkenazic and Sephardic-Turkish marriage contracts (see Glazer 1979), and the amount reflected, and sometimes affected, the social status of the people involved. But in Morocco the Jewish nuclear family was created without such an individual property base. Rather, the property base of the nuclear family was rooted within that of the extended family. It is possible that the total sum, given by kinsmen of both bride and groom to the father of the groom, was considerable. But since neither bridewealth nor dowry were of prime significance, the parents did not need to exert themselves greatly to mobilize resources to permit marriage. The sources do not reflect a situation where marriage presents a great economic burden for parents, as was the case in some other Jewish societies.

The extended patriarchal family remained potent as long as the pater familias remained alive, and also for some time after his death. The family property was, upon the demise of the patriarch, only partly divided among the sons (Elmaleh 43; vol. 2, 112). Half the property remained undivided and was formally owned by the widow, although in practice it was most likely managed jointly by the sons. The sociological implication of this inheritance arrangement is that full economic independence is attained by the nuclear family only upon the death of the widow of the pater familias. Demographic pressure on the extended household must have been considerable for many years before the decease of the parents, because of the growth of the constituent nuclear families. The latter were themselves in the process of becoming extended households, and the original extended household must have begun to disintegrate. The death of the remaining parent, and the ultimate distribution of the joint property, dissolved the household formally.

After the mid-nineteenth century, we have reports from Fez and

Sefrou that the practice of the widow retaining half of the family property upon death of the pater familias was causing disputes among the heirs (S. Ibn-Danan: 146; Ben-Shetrit 8). Henceforth, some courts ruled that the total property be divided among the heirs of the patriarch and that the widow receive only the amount due according to her ketuba agreement. An important conclusion may be drawn from this: the Moroccan Jewish extended family, considered as a corporate property holding group, comprised no more than two generations, father and adult sons. The custom to extend the hold of communal property beyond two generations, through joint holding by the widow, was problematic, and the mid-nineteenth-century Fez sage preferred to abolish it.[14] This does not necessarily preclude the possibility that property was sometimes held jointly by patrilineal kinsmen for more than two generations. With the generation of the adult sons, however, a point is reached at which the hold of the extended family on individuals becomes increasingly problematic and conflict ridden.

Although the nuclear family of the mellah people was part of a wider net of kin, it simultaneously enjoyed a measure of independence. The tension, between independence on the one hand and enclosure within a broader family system on the other hand, sometimes found expression in court. People felt responsibility toward their extended kin. This responsibility or, in sociological terms, the lack of differentiation between the nuclear family and wider circles of kin is evident in the following case: A man wanted to break the engagement to his bride without having to pay the customary penalty. The man contended that after the engagement he had discovered that an aunt of the bride had given birth out of wedlock, and therefore the family of the bride was tainted. The judge cited a precedent in which the sister of a bride had defected from Judaism and where again the side of the groom had rescinded their agreement. The ruling in that case had been in favor of the groom. In the present case, also, the judge therefore ruled in favor of the groom because, he explained, "What does it matter if a sister [of the bride] or an aunt [of the bride] is involved?" (Ibn-Sur 75). The two degrees of kinship are thus considered as one. A similar atmosphere pervades another case that involved Jewish-Muslim relationships. A man was pressed for money by a Muslim. For some undisclosed reason another man paid the Muslim the sum that he claimed. The payer now requested that the first man reimburse him, and the latter refused. One of the arguments he presented in the Jewish court was, "I have relatives and they would have paid for me; then

I would not have had to spend anything" (Abihsera 62). This argument expresses an elemental feeling, that in times of trouble a person expects his kin to come to his assistance, even if that is of material substance.[15]

The case does not include information about the scope of the circle of relatives who are considered obligated, but another case sheds light on that question. Again a man was pressed by Muslims for money, and in the course of extortion he was imprisoned. The problem presented to the Jewish court was, who of the prisoner's relatives was obliged to provide the sums required for extortion and bribes, in order to obtain the man's release? The relatives involved were the prisoner's wife, his wife's father, and his mother's brother. The sage ruled that the obligation of siblings preceded that of in-laws; and he placed prime responsibility in this case on the mother's brother (Ben-Walid 67).[16] These data confirm that family liability was not restricted to the nuclear family but extended to siblings of the parents. On the other hand, we have no indication of family incorporation beyond that range.

The picture that now emerges is one of corporate extended kin relationships that are potent, but only within a restricted range of relatives, namely, that of the closest circle beyond the nuclear family. Other than that we only encountered evidence of kin-related verbosity. We saw people encourage, and dissuade, others to act by having recourse to slogans pertaining to kin-related ideals, such as family honor and the welfare of the souls of dead ancestors. These slogans figured in emotion-charged contexts, and sometimes fired domestic disputes. But viewing the data as a whole, kinship emerges in practice as less potent than one would have expected on the basis of the verbal expressions alone. This conclusion brings us back to the broader setting. In common with Moroccans generally, Moroccan Jews exhibit both deep attachment to cultural norms and vigorous individualism. This led people to develop loyalties individually according to changing situations. Therefore, while ideally kinship was important and valued, in practice it was binding only within a close range of kinsmen.

Coming to the specific role of women in the family, the parallel between Muslim and Jewish Moroccans diverges. Living in the kind of family environment I have described, Jewish women were profoundly secluded within the domestic domain. We have no indication that Jewish women had much bargaining power rooted in the manipulation of individual relationships, as is emphasized in ethnographies of Muslim Moroccan society. Married sexuality was the one area in which Jewish women dominated, and that was the main source of female power, in contrast to the parallel Muslim situation. It is tempting to link the difference in Jewish and Muslim female power with the fact that in Islam the issue of menstrual pollution is less stringent than in Judaism, hence less prone to manipulation in domestic politics (see Mernissi 1975: 25).[17] In precolonial Moroccan Judaism, again in contrast to Islam, the domain of men was not only that of public life and the marketplace, but clearly also that of the home. In mellah society, men had crucial ritual functions to fulfill in the home, so that the household was not relegated to the level of an inferior female domain. The prestigious public domain of religion, in which men operated, intruded into the privacy of the domestic domain, because men had a role in numerous domestic rituals. On the other hand, women had a crucial role in the cultural control of married sexuality, which is parallel to the manipulation of social relationships reported for Muslim Moroccan women. In these areas of domestic activity, the mellah women were afforded some scope for self-assertion in a social environment that was generally repressive.

9 CONCLUSIONS

We have in the course of these chapters discussed the nature of the economy, the self-rule, religious affairs, and family life of Moroccan Jews in Sherifian times. In each of those areas of life, the questions that concerned us were focused on one issue, namely, the tension between the public interest and that of the individual. We sought to uncover the balance whereby mellah society accommodated these contradictory social forces. The tension of the one against the many is present in the societies of many cultures and peoples. But in the Jewish society of precolonial Morocco this tension is particularly salient, because of the general background of Moroccan Islamic culture in the centuries following the maraboutic crisis of the sixteenth century. The history of Morocco since that turmoil has been characterized by the recurrent emergence on the sociopolitical scene of personalities fired by religious inspiration, who claim authority and assert themselves accordingly.

The Jews of Morocco did not undersign this religiopolitical tradition, particularly since their leadership harked back to the sages of medieval Spain, who adhered to their Sephardic religious and social heritage. According to that heritage, primacy was attributed to aristocratic lineages that combined learning, dignity, tradition—all elements far removed from maraboutic-type miracle working, spontaneity, and disorder. However, over time, the *megorashim* from Spain sank into their Moroccan environment, despite their different roots, and despite the communalism that bound them to each other. The megorashim fused with the autochthonous *toshavim* Jews, and all the mellah people lived their lives in an environment that was common to both them and to Muslim Moroccans. Over hundreds of years the lives of Moroccan Jews were molded in a channel that had much in common with that of their Muslim neighbors, though it remained separate.

There developed in Morocco a Jewish society, fueled from both Se-

phardic and autochthonous sources, founded on the tradition of rabbinical learning. But that society also harbored the religiosity of ordinary people which had important components of spontaneity and folk
practices. The most vivid expression of this element in Moroccan
Jewry is the veneration of the burial places of saints and the public
reading of the mystical *Zohar* text (even when divorced from cognitive
understanding). Above, in Chapter 6, we remarked upon the fact that
there are indications of the ongoing and increasing development of
these elements in folk religion. The thrust of the developments is toward an increasing emphasis on the relative power of the individual,
spontaneity and initiative, at the expense of formality and the order of
the community—all far removed from the classical Sephardic tradition.

Many Jewish practices in several areas of life came to be aligned with
the general Moroccan environment. Besides the emergence of saint
veneration, certain specific matters that had long concerned the communities, and over which there had been many disputes, came in time
to be resolved. The trend of the resolutions all point in the direction
that I have indicated, namely, the increasing acceptance of the Moroccan way, and a distancing from Sephardic tradition. One such community concern was the problem of private synagogues. We followed
the increasing tolerance of the mellah people for noncommunal synagogues, a system that dovetailed with the general Moroccan system
but which was foreign to "the sages of Castille" and to those who
adhered to their tradition.

We noted that the eighteenth- and nineteenth-century sages sometimes exaggerated in their beliefs concerning the prevalence and antiquity of private synagogues in the Maghreb. They also seem not to
have always been cognizant of the fact that the type of synagogue-
management prevalent in their time was the outcome of a process of
development; in fact, it was sometimes a quite recent development.
Thus, we learn that in Sefrou, as late as the early eighteenth century,
the judge and prayer leaders used to receive a fixed stipend from the
community, which "the treasurer" collected on their behalf. Only later
was this changed, the officials obtaining the indeterminate accrue-
ments of the community synagogue (Mordekhay Berdugo 28). Sociologically, this indicates a far-reaching process of deinstitutionalization
of community institutions. The roles of the sages and community officials, and the organs which governed the roles in the past, and the
community synagogue—all shed some elements of their differentiated
existence.

Another old community concern in which this trend is evident, is the extension of the rights of owners of private synagogues. Whereas as late as 1750 the Fez sages reiterated the old prohibition against the establishment of private synagogues (Seifer ha'taqanot 177), thereafter they ruled less firmly. The sages now afforded the lay inheritors of synagogues more rights than in the past, and as a result more synagogues came to be managed by powerful lay individuals.[1] We saw that this change entailed an explicit shift, from the Sephardic to the autochthonous practice. A parallel change occurred in family inheritance practices, where again the autochthonous custom reasserted itself. Inherited property in the nineteenth century came to be divided immediately upon the demise of the pater familias, as against the previously prevailing Sephardic practice of continuing joint holding of property until the complete demise of the older generation, that is, the death of the widow of the pater familias. There is another notable change in family law in the nineteenth century. Whereas in the past a childless man was prohibited, according to Sephardic regulation, from taking a second wife before the elapse of ten years of marriage, this was now permitted after five years (S. Ibn-Danan: 145b). We saw (in Chap. 3) that the sages of Morocco were subjected to repeated pressure over this matter. Apparently the Sephardic regulation became unacceptable in time.

The process of detachment from Sephardic practices and the acceptance of autochthonous practices did not begin in the nineteenth century. There are indications to that effect already in the seventeenth century. Thus, the megorashim at that time abandoned their particular practice in favor of that of the toshavim in a certain matter of divorce law, the rights of a divorcee concerning her personal effects (Bentov 1986: 90). But divorces were extraordinary events, and therefore divorce laws affected only a relatively small number of people. During the nineteenth century, however, there is a trend away from Sephardic practice in matters of ordinary and daily concern that affected many people. Namely, the aforementioned matters of synagogue management and routine inheritance practices. These affected ordinary synagogue goers and inheritors of property. Thus, in time, distancing from the Sephardic tradition and acceptance of the autochthonous tradition increasingly entailed changes in matters that were highly salient to people. Moreover, the nature of the changes also indicates an increasing emphasis on the weight of the individual in social life as against the weight of elements that are communal, familial, and formal.

This brings us to the tantalizing question: Why did mellah society develop in this way? At this point, however, we grope in the dark. One possible approach to the problem is deterministic. Namely, that in time the weight of the immediate sociocultural environment, both Muslim and authochthonous Jewish, caused mellah society to distance itself from one of its sources, the alien Sephardic element. Such an approach, by itself, is however superficial; a specific factor that might enrich it is that of demographic change. We noted in several of the foregoing discussions that there are indications of a significant increase of population in the communities in the second half of the nineteenth century.[2] It is sociologically reasonable to assume that such a development will have profound and widespread ramifications.

In discussing the problem of establishing private synagogues, the nineteenth-century sages repeatedly allude to the issue of crowdedness in the existing synagogues. Apparently the pressure of population was salient in the decision making of the community leaders. We have an illuminating observation by a sage in the context of a deliberation about the abandonment of the old Fez practice of sages paying rent to lay synagogue owners. "Rentals in our time have increased," notes the sage (R. M. Elbaz, Orah hayim 9). He argues that the Fez practice, therefore, be abandoned, as it would be detrimental to the material interests of sages. The Marrakesh practice would be more remunerative from the sages' point of view. Increased rentals are a typical result of population expansion. It is, therefore, to the latter that I attribute the shift in the social structure of nineteenth-century mellah synagogues.

Having described in the opening chapters of this study the general structure of political relationships in Sherifian times and the nature of the Jewish economy, I then focused on Jewish self-rule. The disparate features of the latter are not all unique to Moroccan Jewry; they figure in other times and places of the Jewish Diaspora. But although the disparate details are not unique, the entire, complex configuration of features is indeed uniquely Jewish Moroccan. Moreover, this configuration is readily comprehended when viewed against the background setting of Sherifian times. In particular, many of the particular features of mellah society can be readily comprehended when related to the basic material situation of the communities, namely, the salience of long-distance peddling. The individualistic centrifugal elements in the mellah social structure should be seen as ramifications of the material situation. The evidence indicates that mellah society was fractured by ties that linked individual Jews to Muslims, and these ties also had ramifications in internal relationships within mellah society. The mellah situation as a whole was uniquely Moroccan, although some of its specific features were common to other parts of the traditional Jewish diaspora.

The research of social anthropologists and historians on Moroccan towns in the past two decades has uncovered important features of the social networks and of the cultural assumptions within which Moroccans operated. The present study of urban Jews demonstrates that social relationships of the kind extant among the Muslim majority also operated among the Jewish minority. Of the several anthropologists who have contributed to Maghrebi studies in our times, the work of Lawrence Rosen has been particularly stimulating to Maghrebi Jewish studies. He has described Muslim-Jewish relations in a Moroccan town in terms of a general thesis that he articulated, following Geertz (1968). Namely, that relations between individuals in traditional Morocco were governed to a considerable degree by particular person-to-person ties, and to a lesser degree by the abstract social categories into which a person fitted (Rosen 1972, 1984). Thus patron-client ties, forged between an individual Muslim and an individual Jew, were resilient and often impervious to the contrasting ethnic and religious categories that crosscut those ties.

The Rosen thesis has been challenged by the historian Norman Stillman (1977, 1978), who marshaled literary sources that demonstrate the humiliation to which Jews were categorically subjected in traditional Morocco. The crux of the argument was about the relative value of a conflict model, or of an integrationist model in viewing relations between Moroccan Jews and Muslims. While Rosen stressed the integrationist model, Stillman argued in favor of the opposing model. Subsequently, Allan Meyers (1982) proposed that Rosen's thesis was pertinent in those regions of Morocco where the central polity was weak, but in areas where sultanic power was relatively effective the description of Stillman was pertinent. The data of the present study support that contention.

The data also bear on a virtually classic issue of Middle Eastern studies, namely, the clarification of the nature of the traditional so-called "Islamic city." Travelers to Morocco, anthropologists included, have commonly been impressed by the salience of the physical features of the mellahs. The Jewish quarters were clearly distinguishable by their crowdedness and poverty. In fact, to this day, although their erstwhile residents vacated them many decades ago, the old mellahs retain their squalid distinctiveness. On the other hand, in the traditional city, various Muslim quarters and houses were, to paraphrase Eickelman (1981: 270–273), not readily distinguishable externally on the basis of wealth or other criteria. Recent works on the nature of Moroccan cities have begun to uncover the more subtle bonds and demarcations that operate in that setting (Eickelman 1974, Abu-Lughod 1987).

Having uncovered the nature of the social boundaries of mellah society on the basis of internal data, a revision of the conventional view of the mellah as exceptional is called for. The Jews were of course dhimmi, members of an inferior religioethnic minority, who were subordinated, often humiliated, and occasionally persecuted. This particular position of the Jews, however, should not blind us to the fact that they were also Fasis, Sefruwis, Slawis, residents of Fez, Sefrou, Salé, and so forth. They shared with the Muslim majority many common features, notably the amorphous, fluid element prevalent in the general Moroccan social structure. When studying the Jewish community in its urban context, one becomes aware of the presence of this element also in the structure of the community. Patron-client relationships were potent, profoundly affecting the situation of individuals. These relationships also affected the structure of mellah society and the political autonomy of the community. The boundaries of Jewish society, while theoretically clear and defined, were in fact permeable. Jews sometimes moved between the majority and minority societies. Further, intervention from the outside sometimes penetrated the intimacy of domestic and religious affairs of mellah society. This amorphousness of the social structure has a decided Moroccan stamp. The social contours of the Jewish community that emerge are not a marginal exception to what we know of Moroccan social life generally, but rather are consistent with the overall picture.

The purpose of this book was to formulate a thesis and follow it through the major areas of life in mellah society. Its thrust was to conceptualize Moroccan Jewry in a local context. The state of research, particularly the limited sources available, and the thin base of previous research in this field do not permit definitive conclusions. But they do permit a disciplined conceptualization of the available data, and this invites refinement and challenge.

NOTES

Chapter One

1. Of the numerous anthropological works on Maghrebi topics, in which some or all of the forementioned themes figure, I mention a few book-length studies: Evans-Pritchard 1949; Gellner 1969; Geertz 1968; Rosen 1984; Eickelman 1976, 1985a; Brown 1976; Geertz, Geertz, and Rosen 1979; Burke 1976. For two recent reconsiderations of some of the major issues of these studies see Combs-Schilling 1985 and Caton 1987.

2. See Deshen and Zenner 1982 which presents an overview of the state of research on Middle-Eastern Jewries, accompanied with a selection of readings and an annotated bibliography.

3. Similarly, it is only recently that Judaic scholars have become aware of the existence of "the shtetl model" in their thinking (see the critical overview of Kirshenblatt-Gimblett, forthcoming). It is debatable to what extent this model is appropriate in the study of Ashkenazic Jewry, but it is certainly misleading when applied to the study of Middle-Eastern Jewry.

4. Avrom Udowitch has drawn my attention to the Tunisian source of Geniza materials. As to the comparative comments concerning the Jewries of Morocco and Tunisia, juxtapose the chapters by Shokeid and Deshen in the Deshen and Zenner (1982) anthology on Morocco and Tunisia, respectively, and also the material of this monograph on Moroccan Jewry.

5. For an elaboration of this argument see the introductory essay to Deshen and Zenner 1982.

6. For these developments see, beyond the general histories of Morocco, Bowie 1976; Miège 1980; Kenbib 1984; Schroeter, unpublished. An epistle by a Meknes sage in 1882 shows evidence that by that time the authority of the Jewish court was weakened, and the sage was cognizant of the nature of the historical development (S. Amar: 98).

7. This is how an early eighteenth-century sage summarized the situation: "The custom of the *megorashim* is accepted in Fez and all the cities of the Maghreb, except for Tafilalt and its surroundings, while in Marrakesh some do this and some do that (*yeish va'yeish*) (Quriat 75; also Ben-Malka 55)."

8. On the eve of the Spanish expulsion Castille was the Iberian province where Jewry was most vital. Until the 1391 pogroms Aragon had been the major Jewish center, and before that, until the twelfth-century Almohad insurgence, the communities of Andalusia had been preeminent.

125

9. In the 1520s there was a squabble between the toshavim and megorashim rabbis in Fez over a matter of religious custom. Before the megorashim decisively won, the toshavim leader expressed himself pathetically in a memoir, "My force is spent (*kashal koah ha'seivel*), and I am old and weak" (Gaguine 1987: 108).

10. The extent to which the Sephardic element dominated the autochthonous element in Moroccan Jewry is evident in the names by which synagogues in Morocco were known. Whereas in many parts of the Sephardic Diaspora the synagogues were known by ethnic names, recalling the particular locality in Spain or Portugal from which the congregants harked, this was not so in Morocco. Here we find ethnic identities attributed in particular to the autochthonous Jews, hence the Synagogue of the Toshavim in Fez, sometimes even the Synagogue of the Fasis. In small communities that had only one place of worship, synagogues were not usually named. In the larger communities synagogues were often named after founding individuals, or after sages who graced synagogues with their attendance. The Moroccan synagogue-naming practice indicates that the Sephardic element was so deeply entrenched that it was conceived as normative, and anyone who did not have that identity was conceived as ethnically exceptional.

11. Though composed mostly of sixteenth-century material, the Seifer Ha'taqanot codex was collated over the centuries by several sages. In its final format it was brought to press by Avraham Anqawe (1871). Recently it has been reissued by Bar-Asher (1977) and Amar (1980).

12. While indeed there is evidence for the loss of manuscripts (Stahl 1979a), this is not unique to the early period. The nineteenth-century Alexandria publisher of the writings of Rabbi Ya'aqov Ibn-Sur (1673–1753) complains that rats had devoured part of the manuscript (Ibn-Sur, vol. 2, 185). Nevertheless, the material the publisher had on hand sufficed to produce a large two-tome collection. Even the twentieth-century publisher of the writings of a sage who lived just one generation before him complains similarly (H. Meshash: 235, and unpaginated introduction; also Elkhreif: 8b).

13. The consideration to limit the study to the eighteenth and nineteenth centuries is also based on the practical matter of comparatively limited source material available for the earlier period. This is a problem into which Jane Gerber ran in her *Jewish Society in Fez, 1465–1700,* that is, the early period of Sephardic hegemony. Because of the paucity of sources, Gerber was reduced to rely on three major sources only: the Fez chronicle of the Ibn-Danan family (dealing mainly with the misfortunes that afflicted the community), the Seifer ha'taqanot, and the responsa collection of Ibn-Sur. The latter is by far the richest and most illuminating of the three. However, it mostly pertains to the eighteenth century and not to the period that Gerber aims to illuminate.

14. For a comprehensive overview of the historiography of Moroccan Jewry, see Abitbol 1988. The next step to be taken is to study the Arabic sources pertinent to Jews, which are stored in Moroccan archives both of the Sherifian administration and of Muslim academies. It is encouraging that in recent years Moroccan Muslim historians have begun to show an interest in the study of Moroccan Jewry as part of Moroccan history. But to the extent that I have been able to acquaint myself with this work, I am not impressed that it has been greatly informed as yet by the source material that I suggest.

Chapter Two

1. The overview of these paragraphs is founded on the anthropological and historical works mentioned in the introduction, and particularly on Burke 1976; Gellner and Micaud 1973; Jamous 1981, chap. 11.

2. The reason for this development is not very clear, but one particular historical development seems obviously pertinent. That development is the turnover in power relations in the Western Mediterranean in the late Middle Ages. Whereas in earlier times Islam was an aggressive, victorious religious and political force, it had been floundering for centuries in the face of the Spanish *reconquista*. One reaction of Moroccan Muslims to this were the revitalization movements. By the sixteenth century the Spanish Christians had not only obliterated the remnant of Omayad glory in Granada but were beleaguering the Moroccan littoral. The increasing frustration and religious affront, I suggest, elicited ever more frantic religious responses.

3. Of all the 'Alawi sultans, only the two most powerful ones, Ismail ibn-al-Sharif and Mohammed ibn-Abd'allah, of the seventeenth and eighteenth centuries, respectively, did not adopt the title *amir al-mu'minin*. It is tempting to interpret this as follows: These two sultans commanded sufficient material power to enable them to exert authority without having recourse to the problematic and double-edged religious legitimization. But as the period of European imperialistic incursion loomed close, in the nineteenth century, and the actual power of the sultans evaporated, they were reduced to insist more and more on their religious legitimization (see Meyers 1977 who develops this thesis).

4. Recent research has uncovered details of the relationship prevailing between the ulama and other Moroccan religious role bearers. The picture that emerges is that "far from being in opposition to urban-based scholars, many marabouts were respected by them and shared similar notions of Islam, even though popular understandings of their role were often at variance with 'formal' Islamic precepts" (Eickelman 1981: 233; see also the whole of his discussion of maraboutism there, and references to specialized studies, particularly Eickelman 1985a). Also see Brown 1972 and Burke 1972.

5. For a dramatic example of this in our own times, see the account of events surrounding the attempted overthrow of King Hassan by rebellious military personnel in 1971 (Waterbury 1973).

6. In North Africa, ever since Islam obliterated Christianity, there remained no religious minority other than the Jewish, hence the term "dhimmi" came to be synonymous with "Jew."

7. For discussions of the term see Hirschberg 1956; and Brown 1981.

8. Our knowledge of conditions in the tribal areas is sketchy due to the paucity of sources. Also, anthropologists who worked in those areas evinced less interest in the Jewish minority than did those who worked in the urban areas. But the information that we do have reflects conditions of dyadic patron-client relationships, such as is reported for the towns. David Hart, whose work on tribal areas is probably the most detailed available, reports language usages in southern Morocco vis-à-vis Jews that are illuminating. The Jews had Berber patrons and addressed them as "my lord." The patrons spoke of their clients as "my Jew" and "our Jews," and are reported to have had the practice of "selling" them to each other (Hart 1984: 125–127).

9. The common participation of Jews and Muslims at these rituals is far re-

moved from comparable modern interfaith activities. The traditional Moroccan rituals do not reflect liberal tolerance of religious diversity; rather, they reflect what symbolic anthropologists would now term "the power of the weak." This is well expressed in a Muslim rationalization for the participation of Jews in joint petitions for rain, that God cannot tolerate the foul odor of the Jews' breath and feet, and therefore their requests are granted promptly (cited in Bar-Asher 1980).

10. This intimacy, too, should, however, be seen within the overall context of Muslim-Jewish patron-client relationships. Acting as an intermediary in matchmaking is a socially weighty undertaking. The intermediary stakes his reputation in case of failure, because he causes embarrassment to the party whom he represents. Availing oneself of the matchmaking services of one's Muslim patron should, therefore, be seen as more than an act of altruistic friendship; it should be seen also as a calculated sociopolitical gesture, in a matter that is weighty with social ramifications (see Eickelman 1976: 148–149).

11. This conception is pervasive among Middle-Eastern Jews and has further ramifications. Thus, a nineteenth-century Jerusalem sage, Rabbi Avraham Ashkenazi (the name reflects a Sephardic, probably Balkan background), writes that "the Arabic language is corrupt Hebrew" (cited in Bashan 1982).

12. The Hebrew term is probably intended as a play of words on the Arabic term *fqih*, usually referring to a minor scholar (such as a Quranic teacher or literate person).

13. Shalom Bar-Asher (1980) goes so far as to take the source as evidence for actual interfaith tolerance, which I doubt. I tend to view the account as fictive, because it is difficult to conceive of the Muslim disputant leaving downcast and the Jewish partner triumphantly writing about the incident. Challenging Islam was apt to lead to heavy monetary fines, and sometimes to corporal and even capital punishment. At least one might have expected a rabbi, who came out of such an encounter, to express himself piously, in terms of divine salvation. Also, the style of the account is unusual. Normally, writers such as P. Berdugo record carefully the wordings of individuals who figure in litigations, so much that they frequently shift between languages and styles. The present account, however, is florid and polished. Passages that are purported to be direct quotations lack the stamp of live conversation. I, therefore, suggest that we have here a literary composition, according to the conventional model of a medieval religious dispute, and it should be evaluated as such.

14. The major exception to this generalization is late medieval Spanish Jewry, after the reconquista, which saw mass defections to Christianity. Historians have explained this by certain factors that are specific to that society. For a recent summary see Sharot 1982, chap. 5.

15. The patron-client relationship could also be of benefit to the community. We hear of a synagogue that was spared during an insurgency, because of an individual "who was the Jew of the governor (*ha'sar*), and he stood fast and said that the synagogue belonged to him" (Ovadia 1979: 39).

Chapter Three

1. In a fine dissertation on the nineteenth-century port city of Essaouira, Daniel Schroeter (1984b) has documented meticulously these natural calamities. Of the misfortunes of individuals, we have on hand the history of Ibn-Sur, the eighteenth-

century sage. He fathered seventeen children, all of whom, with the exception of one boy, he buried in his lifetime (M. Amar 1981: 99).

2. Traditional Jewry tolerates a variety of practices in this matter. Ashkenazic Jewry forbids polygamy totally. In cases of prolonged childlessness it recommends easy divorce procedures and remarriage to another woman. Middle-Eastern Jewry that follows neither Sephardic nor Ashkenazic custom is lenient toward polygamy. Thus among Yemenite immigrants to Israel who married abroad I have encountered families of two, and even of three, wives. Currently, in Israel, the Ashkenazic practice is legally binding on all (Arusi 1986).

3. Thus the Sefrou community leaders, in seeking to regulate the visits of itinerant beggars to the town, order that no solicitation will be permitted unless the visitor has first imposed himself upon the communities of Fez and Meknes. Further, the Sefrou elders rule that the people of the community need give only one-third of what the visitor succeeded in collecting in each of the neighboring communities (Ovadia 43).

4. The same source also reports that there were conversions in Marrakesh in 1613, but no figure is cited, and Corcos (1976: 103) reports of conversions in Rabat in the early nineteenth century. However, not all conversions were permanent. Some people lived as crypto-Jews, and we hear of converts who considered returning to Judaism (Ovadia 6; Bentov 1980: n. 60).

5. The mild attitude toward cases of conversion contrasts with the harsh attitude toward parallel cases of adultery. A sage explains this by the fact that conversions lead to exclusion from the family, but adultery, particularly illicit births, takes place within the family as the immediate kin try to keep the matter secret. There is, therefore, a greater chance of sexual offenders becoming a role model for people in the family and community (Ibn-Sur 75). The data are readily comprehensible through current theories in symbolic anthropology.

6. I suspect this is a misprint and that the original manuscript read *adnei ha'sadeh*, which is a more familiar phrase than that of the text. The word *adnei* also fits perfectly into the wordplay of the text.

Chapter Four

1. We encounter the institution of "the seven elders" occasionally in Sefrou cases (Ovadia 422; vol. 4, 31, 56). We encounter it also in Tetuan, hedged with the proviso that the enactments of the seven elders are binding upon the public only if they "were appointed with the agreement of all the community" (as against self-appointment, or the appointment by only a section of the population) (Ben-Walid, vol. 2, 170). It is hard to conceive that universal agreement to an appointment could have been very common in a large community such as Tetuan. Therefore, I conclude that the institution of "the seven elders" was not vital (as is also explicit in Khalfon 31). Bar-Asher (1981: 73), studying the usage of the analogous concept *ma'amad*, independently reached a similar conclusion. He found that the concept "individual," which was rarely used before the eighteenth century, becomes common thereafter, while the concept ma'amad, that was frequently used during the earlier period, now falls into disuse. There is also explicit evidence to that effect in a statement of a late nineteenth century Meknes sage who cites a manuscript source of Ibn-Sur (H. Meshash: 251).

2. The reason probably is that the Muslims were concerned with the competition. In the course of Jewish slaughtering, some carcasses are declared ritually unfit and must therefore be sold to non-Jewish consumers, often at a low price. Having the Jewish slaughterer work near Muslim customers eased the latter's access to bargain buys.

3. In late Ashkenazic usage, the concept *talmid hakham* has the connotation of a mature scholar (and *hakham* is rarely used), but that is not so in Sephardic usage. Also, the text conveys the fact that talmid hakham is inferior to hakham.

4. This general statement figures with minor differences also in the writings of a thirteenth-century Spanish sage, and it figures in print as an appendix to Azulay (1795). This leads to the possibility that the statement does not reflect an actuality, but a desirability mouthed legalistically by one generation of jurists after the other. However, the factuality of lay adjudication is attested to by the specific cases that I recount presently.

5. The mention of jailing arouses questions as to the nature of imprisonment facilities in the communities. Both in Meknes and Fez we hear of men who refused court orders to grant divorces to their wives and being threatened with incarceration (Ibn-Sur 18; Maimon Berdugo, Even ha'ezer 148). There is also an indication of the nagid in Marrakesh having the power to incarcerate offenders (Deverdun, vol. 2: 562). Also, sixteenth- and seventeenth-century Fez sources in Seifer ha'taqanot report to that effect. However, the sources do not elaborate whether these were community facilities or part of the Muslim penal system. I venture to hypothesize that they were all Muslim facilities, because, as we shall see in detail, the communal facilities were altogether few. In addition, the Moroccan political system led to a situation where community leaders could make use of the executive arm of their Muslim-patron potentates. Moreover, it is unlikely that Muslim governors would permit their dhimmi clients to have their own penitential facilities.

6. The payment of community fines to "the poor" constitutes payment to the one clearly institutionalized monetary fund that the Moroccan communities maintained. It served the needs of both the local poor and outsiders. Occasionally one even encounters needy Ashkenazic people who came to collect charity in the communities. And of course emissaries from Eretz-Yisrael came regularly. More remarkable is the payment to "the rulers." This type of fine is part of the asymmetry of the Jewish polity on which we dwelt in Chapter 2. The practice is based on the fact that the Jewish authorities lacked an executive arm to enforce their will and relied on the non-Jewish authorities for that service. By stipulating that the ruler benefit from the fines of wrongdoers, the Jewish authorities entrenched the vested interest of the non-Jewish authorities in the orderly self-government of the communities. In general, the practice is to be found in many Jewish societies, but the details—such as whether part or all the fines went to the rulers, when, where and under what conditions—remain to be clarified.

7. Because of this paucity of sources we know little of the legal process whereby lay justice was delivered (in contrast to the vast material on this issue pertaining to rabbinical justice that we have on hand for all Jewish societies). Ibn-Sur voices his opinion that a nagid may mete out punishment only after a due process of law that included "witnesses and prior warning" (Ibn-Sur, vol. 2, 63). But that is a classical halakhic formula, and the sage may only have been expressing an ideal.

8. The primary monetary request that was directed toward Jewish communities throughout Muslim lands was the *jizya,* poll tax or head tax. Originally this tax was levied from each dhimmi person on an individual basis and thus permitted the Muslim believers to tolerate the infidels in their midst. But already in the Middle Ages the poll tax began to lose some of its theological ramifications, and the potentates levied it solely to satisfy their rapacity. In this context it became communal. Each community, through its representative—the nagid, *sheikh al-yahud, ca'id,* or however he was termed—delivered payment to its local potentate. Payment of the poll tax, however, retained some theological underpinnings, through the Islamic Middle Ages and to Sherifian times in Morocco, by the symbols of humiliation that remained attached to it. Bernard Lewis (1984: 14–15) quotes the words of a medieval jurist: "When [the dhimmi] pays, he shall stand, while the tax collector sits. The collector shall seize him by the scruff of the neck, shake him, and say: 'Pay the *jizya!'* and when he pays he shall be slapped . . ." Lewis adds: A piece of symbolism prescribed in many law books is that the dhimmi's hand must be below, the tax-collector's hand above, when the money changes hands.

9. Elsewhere Ibn-Sur (249) writes about a powerful individual and tax evasion: ". . . and had he wanted not to pay any tax at all, he could have done so, and he would not have been reviled in the least (*lo haya . . . genay kelal*). For that is the practice of all [those] who are close to the rulers and the negidim. And who can tell him what to do . . . ?"

10. Here is a Meknes example of behavior on the part of a local nagid, who is completely subservient to a local despot: "The [Muslim] governor libelled four men, and ordered them to be imprisoned . . . He then sent his servant and the nagid . . . to search for them" (Maimon Berdugo, Hoshen mishpat 250).

11. We have on hand a rather moving declaration by a newly appointed Sefrou nagid. The man had first tried to evade accepting the office, saying, "I am a craftsman. I am unable to move about engaging in public affairs. I am incompetent, I am inexperienced." For some reason the community insisted, and thereupon the candidate requested that 'a treasurer' be appointed "so that I remain untainted of theft and injustice, and you should not say about me in the future, 'He filled his belly with the holy [endowments] of Israel!'" (Ovadia 1975–1985, vol. 4, 15).

12. The independence of sages to act in appointments comes out in the following remarkable case. A Sefrou nagid had incurred expenses in the course of exercising his duties, but the community people were lax in reimbursing him. The nagid thereupon approached the sage who had certified his appointment, and the latter paid him out of his own pocket. The sage then turned to the community and demanded to be reimbursed (Ovadia 5).

13. Ownership by the community, like ownership by individual Jews, implied the right of rental and transference of the property (*hazaqa*). This was distinct from ownership of the property itself. The latter type of ownership usually remained vested in the Muslim landlord. But the highly intricate system of letting and subletting among the Jews, which entailed diffuse rights for the person in actual occupation, caused the ultimate ownership of the land and buildings to lack much practical content. The subtenant paid rent not only to the landlord but also to the owner of the hazaqa. Further, the hazaqa rules often prohibited subtenants from establishing direct contact with landlords. This also stymied landlords from placing the rental of prop-

erties in the market, as many potential renters were prohibited from encroaching on the rights of the tenants. The effect, in short, was that there was no significant free market for landed property in the mellah.

Chapter Five

1. The aguna status, when a woman's spouse has disappeared without leaving a trace, prohibits her remarriage indefinitely. The sages were at all times concerned to avert this situation.

2. The case that arose in Rabat in 1787 concerned an individual who had evaded payment of a community tax on an unspecified kind of goods that he had imported to the city. The community desired to punish the offender, but lacking the organs to do so it sought the assistance of the Muslim authorities. However, since the regulation the man had broken was itself illicit, the community accused the man of another offense which in fact he had not committed. The particular accusation is illuminating in the context of Muslim-Jewish relationships. The community testified that the offender "had cursed Moses our Master." That in terms of Jewish law is not an offense at all, but in terms of Islamic law it is, and the Muslim authorities acted accordingly. I have elaborated on the case in my Hebrew monograph (1983: 92–93).

3. The following remarks, in a letter by Ibn-Sur, reflect how much the Eretz Yisrael emissaries were cherished in the communities they visited. The letter was written in Fez in 1752, after a long period of unrest that had prevented emissaries from coming.

> To the emissary from Hebron . . . We have taken to heart that for these many years, more than twenty-four years, the emissaries from Eretz-Yisrael have not come . . . And during all those years we craved, ex-pected, waited—when at last will an emissary for the misva [of suport-ing the sages of Eretz-Yisrael], come to us from the holy cities, [so that we may] receive him as one would receive an angel of God. And we would bless [God] for doing superlative good to us, and for keeping us alive [for that event]. And now, when the forementioned sage came to us, we rejoiced with extreme joy. We rejoiced no end. And we exerted ourselves, and we urged each other to assist significantly—in honor of our holy ancestors who are buried in Hebron . . . and we contribute, as if it were a sacrifice to God, the amount of 1500 uqiyot. (Ovadia 1979, vol. 2: 317)

4. These comments on synagogue activities are based primarily on my obser-vations of contemporary life among Moroccan Jews in Israel. I assume the contem-porary practices to have ancient roots. For elaborate descriptions see Shokeid 1971.

Chapter Six

1. These sages are sometimes referred to as *hakhamim reshumim*. The rather obscure term might be understood as "official sages."

2. Occasionally the community supported the part-time scholars by making them beneficiaries of rents that the community received from property that it owned (Ovadia 629). But such support was unreliable, because the communities had no system to ensure the stable flow of income of this kind. There was no mechanism to

rectify default of payment, as the *hazaqa* system caused ownership to become increasingly diffuse, and to be invested in the actual users of the property.

3. The economic ramifications of the rabbinical role in Morocco, that will be elaborated presently, made the threat hollow; there are no indications that it was ever practiced. The threat reflects the situation of traditional Jewry when religious leadership was deeply embedded in ongoing community life. This is in contrast to religions that entertain monasticism of various kinds, and to contemporary Jewry where the differentiation of religious elites from laymen is increasingly pronounced (see Deshen 1978).

4. To my embarrassment I have lost this reference and have failed so far in my efforts to retrieve it.

5. Such occured in a celebrated eighteenth-century case involving rivalry between Ibn-Sur and Rabbi Ya'aqov Ben-Malka over a Fez judicial position. Some of the people involved sought out the nagid of Meknes to intervene on their behalf (M. Amar 1981).

6. In the context of Jewish societies, Moroccan Jewry constitutes an extreme case in the continuity of rabbinical families. In other Jewish societies, such as in the Yemen and in Ashkenazic Europe before the eighteenth century, there is far less evidence of this kind.

7. For a stimulating comparative commentary, placing the Moroccan practice in broader perspective, see Katz 1979. The Moroccan ordination practice is similar to the Babylonian one of geonic times, whereas Ashkenazic practice is similar to that of ancient Eretz Israel. This datum dovetails with a thesis of Jewish history that many Ashkenazic and Sephardic practices differ according to the roots of the two Jewish societies, in Eretz Israel and in Babylonia, respectively.

8. The situation is very different from that of traditional, late medieval Ashkenazic Jewry, where the educational system and the rabbinical manpower market were highly differentiated. Ashkenazic scholars did not study in their family orbits, and not even in their own communities; nor did the communities appoint rabbis from among their own members. Also, the phenomenon of rabbinical lineages was foreign there. Such became common only in the nineteenth century as a result of the incipient breakdown of traditional society.

9. For this insight I have been inspired by Moshe Shokeid's study of Moroccan immigrants in a cooperative village in Israel. Shokeid (1971) dwelt on the usage of the term *va'ad* (committee) in reference to individual committee members. In the culture of these villagers, individuals are seen as congruent with the institution, and the institution as such is not clearly conceptualized as an entity in itself. Shokeid provides rich ethnographic documentation to substantiate this thesis. Extending this thesis, the disparate historical data become intelligible and internally consistent.

10. The last judge of that court was Rabbi Moshe Malka, who is the present Sephardic chief rabbi of Petah-Tiqva in Israel. His voluminous published responsa reflect, in particular, the work of that court.

11. R. Yoseif Berdugo (1802–1854) of Meknes is an exception. He laments that "judges have become like craftsmen" and receive payment from their clients. He would like judges to receive a salary. But it is clear from his comments that this is wishful thinking (Yoseif Berdugo I, 1922–1943, vol. 2: 15).

12. The main figure in the Sefrou cases is the colorful Abitbul whom we encountered earlier in this chapter.

13. See Deshen 1982 and Katz 1961a for southern Tunisian and Ashkenazic Jewry, respectively, where other pertinent practices were developed.

14. In studying these letters one must distinguish between their two parts, the actual message and the introduction in which the addressee is named. The introductory part is always extremely florid, the expressions being mostly stock phrases of praise taken from the many layers of Jewish literature (biblical, Talmudic, medieval), in both Hebrew and Aramaic. Frequently the phrases are arranged according to poetical conventions of the Sephardic tradition, and these determine much of the content. A study of the introductions, which are often very long, close to the length of the message part of the letters, is a desideratum. But this requires much literary expertise. Failing that one is prone to fall into the standard mistake of historians working with rabbinical texts, of imputing reality to vacuous stock phrases. In my comments, I restrict the analysis solely to the message part of the letters and do not venture into the introductory part.

15. The Meknes sources reflect more developed saint veneration than those of other communities, of which we have parallel documentation. It is tempting to speculate on the question as to why this should be so. The phenomenon may be linked to one overt sociological datum. The Meknes sages were particularly creative and learned and belonged to long rabbinical lineages, more than the sages of other communities. Perhaps their standing in their own eyes and in that of laymen led to the relatively early development of saint veneration in Meknes. Altogether the veneration of saints is a well-known Moroccan theme. Issachar Ben-Ami (1984) has produced documentation for no less than about 700 Jewish saints venerated in Morocco (see also Moghrabi 1968; Noy 1964; Stahl 1980). Although the sources of traditional times indicate such activities (Ovadia 119, 190; Ben-Naim: 111), these are mostly of the nineteenth century. The veneration practices seem to have expanded later, toward the end of the nineteenth century (Schroeter 1984a), and much more so during protectorate times. The protocols of rabbinical gatherings in mid-twentieth century contain reservations about the graveside celebrations (M. Amar 1980: 226–228; see also Deshen and Shokeid 1974: 111–113).

16. The ruling of this sage goes further: a layman (*'am ha'ares*) whose father was a sage (*talmid hakham*), and who insulted a peer of nondistinguished lineage, by calling him 'fool-son-of-a-fool' (*shoteh ben shoteh*), is not punishable (Yoseif Berdugo I, 1922–1943: 42). Presumably, the differential status of the sage is potent in reference to the comparable lay ancestor of another person, even after death.

17. In traditional times there are indications only of Rabbi Yehuda Ben-Atar, who possibly may have attained legendary status in his lifetime (Ovadia 1979: 116). Presently, however, as Moroccan saint veneration has developed on to the late twentieth century, the attainment of legendary status has greatly accelerated. Currently, miraculous tales of living Moroccan sage-saints recur commonly.

18. The eighteenth-century Hassidic movement of Eastern European Jewry has several features that are analogous to the phenomenon of Moroccan saint veneration, including that of hereditary charisma and the imputation of theurgic powers to the saint. But there are also important differences, such as the fact that Hassidism is a very self-conscious religious movement that developed a sophisticated theology of its

own to underpin its particular practices, whereas Moroccan saintliness is characterized by folk piety and profounder innocence.

Chapter Seven

1. I entertain an old fascination with synagogue sociology and produced what
may have been the first contribution to the topic in modern ethnography (Deshen
1970, 1972). During the 1970s there appeared several important works that greatly
illuminated the field (primarily Heilman 1976; Shokeid 1971; Loeb 1978).

2. For a typical case of exaggeration of the importance of synagogues, see Tuito
1982, who studied education in precolonial Morocco.

3. Thus Ibn-Sur writes to a bookdealer: "In this country (medina), whenever
people learn that any sage obtained a new book, they all come to borrow it—the
great and the little ones—until the book gets . . . torn and falls apart." The writer
goes on to request the dealer to see to it that the goods are sent to him discreetly
(Ovadia 631). From as late a time as 1867 we hear that Talmud volumes were scarce
(Ovadia 499).

4. This source comes from a Tetuan sage. We hear that teachers in that region
had difficulties finding premises for themselves, as people avoided renting to them
by requesting inordinately high rents. Also, Rabbi Hayim Meshash reports this for
Meknes. Many teachers were reduced to work in their own homes. The lack of differentiation of home from school premises sometimes led to the role of pupil being
fuzzy. We thus hear of a teacher's wife and her neighbors who sometimes use the
schoolchildren to assist them in their homemaking. In Sefrou, on the other hand, in
the nineteenth century when the population increased, we hear that teachers did
operate in synagogues (R. M. Elbaz 8; Y. Ovadia: 20).

5. Of the practice of Zohar-reading circles in domestic settings, there is only
scant indication in our sources. The earliest I encountered are of the late nineteenth
century. My statements are rooted in observations of Moroccan immigrants in Israel
in the 1950s at the time of mass immigration, and I presume that the practices
observed at that time are of ancient origin. The point requires further study.

6. Sociologically, the development of the Sefrou yeshiva parallels that of the
charity organization described in Chapter 5.

7. For an insight into the cultural and social importance of hymn making in
Morocco see Amzallag 1984 and Seroussi 1984. The following is characteristic of
mellah religioaesthetic sensitivities. In a sermon on repentance delivered on the Day
of Atonement, replete with lofty symbols and sentiments, the sage calls on his congregation "to take care of the co-ordination of voice (lishmor 'al hashva'at ha'qol) . . .
for the [lack of] co-ordination of voice is one of the things that prevents prayer so
that it does not reach Him, blessed be He" (Yoseif Berdugo II: 226).

8. See in this connection the pertinent sources cited in Chapter 3, and also
sources cited in Bar-Asher 1980, n. 45. The citation of S. Y. Abitbul in the latter
should be corrected to vol. 2 instead of vol. 1.

9. During the eighteenth and nineteenth centuries, very few synagogues were
established by the public, rather they were established by individuals. We have on
hand a rare case from Debdou, in the early eighteenth century, where apparently the
public established a new synagogue and appointed a sage to manage it. After two
years the people of the community wanted to dismiss him and appoint another sage.

But they discovered that the law was against them, for immediately upon appointment the sage acquired his position for life, and his heirs were entitled to inherit it (Ibn-Sur 19).

10. Such was the case of the centuries' old Bibas synagogue in Tetuan in the nineteenth century. Local tradition had it: "Originally it was . . . of the community." The community had, upon the synagogue's foundation, appointed the first sage of the Bibas family, but thereupon the rule, "After arising he shall not descend," applied to that sage and to his descendants (Ben-Walid, vol. 2, 103).

11. The principle we encountered in the management of synagogues operates also in other religious institutions of the mellah. Thus, the ritual baths (*miqvaot*) were not community institutions available as a service to the public. Rather, they were private, inherited property, available for use for a fee (Ben-Walid, vol. 2, 30; Ibn-Sur 6). Ovadia (124) mentions initiatives of individuals, who allocated themselves suitable spots for bathing along the river that flowed past the Sefrou Jewish quarter. Thereby they established private miqvaot, which were legally protected by the statutes of hazaqa holding (see Chap. 4, n. 13).

12. See Chapter 2, where I dwelt in another context, that of sociopolitical relationships, on the significance of properly responding to the prayers of the cantor.

13. The present analysis implies that the ruling discussed originates in the late eighteenth century; that it is not of ancient provenance cited unacknowledged from old sources. However, in Chapter 4, note 4, discussing the practice of incarcerating tax evaders (cited in Elkhreif 11), I did not assume this. I suggested there that the custom was not of contemporary provenance, but older. I discovered in fact that it originated at least as far back as the thirteenth century, and I offer the pertinent source. The differing assumptions that I bring to these problematic sources require a word of explanation. Namely, the text concerning tax evaders (in Chap. 4) is presented in the eighteenth century sources as a custom (*minhag*) and that hints at ancient provenance. The text discussed here concerning mobility between synagogues is presented as a ruling (*taqana*). This suggests a more recent provenance. If the ruling was ancient, the late citers would have tried to bolster its legitimacy by naming the revered legislators of the past (as is the practice of the copiers of ancient rulings in Seifer Ha'taqanot).

14. In another case of this type, adjudicated by the same judge, the conclusion is similar: in a synagogue in the community of Azamour there officiated a cantor who had inherited the position, but who was not properly qualified. Ordinarily the man should have stepped down in favor of a qualified sage, but he refused to do so. Thereupon the sage ruled that the opponents of the cantor were permitted to secede and establish their own synagogue (R. Berdugo, 1891, pt. 2, 125).

15. Ibn-Sur states matter-of-factly, ". . . as is the practice of all prayer-leaders, who build synagogues for themselves, to enjoy them all their lives" (Ibn-Sur 57; see also Moshe Berdugo: 6b).

16. I venture a speculation as to the possible nature of this concern. In view of the well-documented, powerful hold of the discredited Sabbatian movement in Morocco, people may easily have suspected each other of secret adherence to the heresy.

Chapter Eight

1. The report does not specify the definition of the family. Given the relatively large number of families, and the concept that we may presume nineteenth-century

French officials entertained about the family, it is plausible that the report refers to nuclear families.

2. For Essaouira we have some precise data. In the 1870s the mellah extended to about 12 percent of the area of the town, while its inhabitants amounted to nearly 40 percent of the overall population (Schroeter 1984b: 416). The congestion in Essaouira may have been exceptional due to the particularly large proportion of Jews in the town, but crowdedness was, judging by the travelers' reports, common in other mellahs too (see Montbard 1894: 148–149).

3. Among rabbinical families in particular we have positive evidence of local endogamy (Bentov 1986: 91). For other types of families the evidence on the subject is scanty, but there is no reason to assume that it was different.

4. The judge eventually supported the claim of the bride because of other, more compelling considerations, but he did not specifically reject this particular argument of the defendant.

5. The text is ambiguously phrased. It might also be read as permitting the woman to visit her parents on the Sabbath day.

6. Some of the phrases describing this husband's domestic regime are stock phrases that can be traced back to the twelfth-century codex of Maimonides (Marriage Law XIII, 11). The element that is original and authentic of mellah society is the request to obtain written permission, and that lends vitality and reality to this husband's order. Otherwise one might consider it in the context of an idignant, but not meaningful, repetition of precedent.

7. Similar principles governed socializing among men. The variegated and rich activities of both the synagogue and the market, however, offered the men a much wider scope for socializing than the women. In traditional times socializing per se, in a context other than religious or economic, was not approved. Moreover, even social visiting on Sabbaths and festivals was frowned upon by the sages in a discussion of heads of households who used to go visiting at inappropriate times. The sages, in seeking to discourage the practice, reminded visitors that they were "subordinating" themselves to their hosts (Ovadia 46).

8. Among latter-day Moroccan Jews in Israel, the common term for the women's synagogue section is 'azara, gallery or section. I have come across the term yeshiva shel ha'nashim, "sitting-place of the women" (Ovadia 1979: 38).

9. Such a case figures in a marriage agreement, where matrilocality is coupled with an undertaking on the part of the bride's father to support the groom for as long as he devotes himself to Torah study. This kind of arrangement, common in traditional Ashkenazic Jewry, was rare in Morocco. But in that exceptional case it was understood that a man who undertook the unusual burden of supporting a son-in-law was entitled to the satisfaction, pleasure, and honor, of having him in his entourage. People would see him deferred to by a scholarly son-in-law. The situation is also explained by the particularly tender age of the bride, and her parents were reluctant to permit a patrilocal arrangement (Maimon Berdugo, Hoshen mishpat 210; also Ibn-Sur 181).

10. On this point we have general evidence. A sage discussing the extent to which men who work outside their homes are involved in domestic affairs, writes: "We see that a husband does not know what articles (keilim ve'hafasim) he has in his home, except for some particular articles." And he adds a personal note: "I myself am domiciled at home at all times, summer and winter, yet in spite of this, I have no

idea how many shirts and trousers I own" (M. Toledano: 42). The sage implies that people who are not as sedentary as scholarly rabbis are even less knowledgeable in these domestic matters.

11. Characteristic of the overall Judeo-Moroccan situation is one case, where brothers of a married woman are reported as having involved additional people in a domestic dispute. But those are Muslim potentates, not kinsmen (Ovadia 406).

12. I report on this practice from latter-day Israeli experience and have not seen mention of it in historical sources. I assume that the custom is traditional.

13. In one marriage agreement (Ovadia 508) we find the father of a bride stipulating that the father of the groom give the wedding gifts to his son the groom. The matter was evidently not self-understood. This agreement contains clauses that are particularly favorable to the young couple, such as that they would be completely maintained by the father of the groom ("Of his bread he will eat, and out of his cup he will drink") for the duration of no less than five years. These clauses are probably linked to the fact that the father of the bride was a sage and his daughter still immature.

14. It is reasonable to assume that also before the mid-nineteenth century property was sometimes divided fully upon death of the pater familias. I base this assumption on the fact that the sources, while replete with legal proceedings involving wills and inheritances, report of very few cases involving the supposed nineteenth-century change. If the change had been very drastic, one would have expected many more litigations stemming from objections to the new rule, on the part of people to whom it was foreign and who stood to lose by it. In the nineteenth century, however, we encounter awareness and consciousness of these matters, and that is a point of importance I discuss in the conclusion.

15. The court eventually judged in favor of the payer, because of other more compelling considerations, but it did not specifically reject the particular argument of the defendant concerning kinship.

16. From another sage, we hear that maternal relatives are liable only in case of exceptional need. Normally, the liability of paternal kin is primary (M. Toledano: 42). In any case, liability is not restricted to the nuclear family.

17. The relatively lenient Muslim view of female pollution might be linked with the highly articulated and clear-cut image of women in the worldview of Islam, in contrast to many other cultures in which the position of women is not defined so unambiguously. The theory of Mary Douglas (1966), concerning the role of body symbols in conceptual boundary maintenance, might be illuminating here.

Chapter Nine

1. The change is prone to a misinterpretation. One might consider it in terms of democratization, as if according to the autochthonous Marrakesh custom greater weight is attributed to the will of the lay members of the congregation than according to the Sephardic Fez custom. Such an interpretation would be anachronistic, reflecting latter-day concerns that are not pertinent to our field. In fact, according to both customs, the public carries little weight in governing institutions. It is characteristic that even Rabbi Yishaq Ben-Walid, a Tetuan sage who adopted the Marrakesh custom, expresses himself disdainfully about lay congregants who sought to have a say in the running of their synagogue. He rules that if lay congregants are not pleased with their prayer leader "let them go wherever they fancy" (Ben-Walid, vol. 2: 85b).

2. Schroeter (1984b) develops the thesis that population increase was only moderate when considered in the context of the dramatic growth of other comparable Middle Eastern cities. However, in mellah society even a comparatively limited expansion would have major effects due to the fundamental crowdedness of the Jewish quarters.

REFERENCES

Abihsera, Ya'aqov. *Yoru mishpatekha le'ya'aqov*. Jerusalem: 1885.

Abitbol, Michel. "Toledot yehudey sefon-afriqa ba'eit ha'hadasha ba'historiografia ha'kelalit ve'ha'yehudit." Pp. 209–222 in *Iyunim be'historiografia*, edited by Moshe Zimmerman, Menahem Stern, and Yoseif Salmon. Jerusalem: Shazar Center, 1988.

Abitbul, Sha'ul Yeshu'a. *Avnei shayish*. 2 vols. Jerusalem: 1935.

Abu-Lughod, Janet. "The Islamic City: History, Myth, Islamic Essence, and Contemporary Relevance." *International Journal of Middle East Studies* 19 (1987): 155–176.

Amar, Moshe. *Ha'mishpat ha'ivri bi'qehilot maroqo*. Mevaseret Yerushalayim: Toledot, 1980.

———. "Qavim li'demuto shel rabbi ya'aqov ibn-sur." *Mi'mizrah u'mi'ma'arav* 3 (1981): 89–124.

Amar, Shemuel. *Devar shemuel*. Casablanca: 1940.

Amzallag, Avraham. "Ha'qasida be'shir yedidot: ha'meqorot, ha'teqst ve'ha'musiqa." *Pe'amim* 18 (1984): 88–112.

Anqawe, Avraham. *Kerem hemer*. 2 vols. Leghorn: 1869–1871.

Anqawe, Refael. *Qarney re'em*. Jerusalem: 1910.

———. *To'afot re'em*. Casablanca: 1930.

Arusi, Rason. "Poseqey yameinu nokhah rav-goniut adatit." Pp. 65–105 in *Mahasit ha'uma*, edited by Shlomo Deshen. Ramat-Gan: Bar-Ilan University, 1986.

Attal, Robert. "Al ha'defus ha'ivri be'maroqo." *Mi'mizrah u'mi'ma'arav* 2 (1980): 121–130.

Azulay, Hayim Yoseif David. *Hayim sha'al*. Leghorn: 1795.

Baer, Yitzhak. "Ha'yesodot ve'ha'hathalot shel irgun ha'qehila ha'yehudit bi'ymey ha'beinayim." *Zion* 15 (1950): 1–41.

Bar-Asher, Shalom, ed. *Taqanot yehudey maroqo*. Jerusalem: Shazar Center, 1977.

———. "Ha'yahasim ha'hevratiyim bein yehudim le'vein sevivatam: pereq be'toledot yehudey maroqo ba'meia ha-18." Pp. 217–237 in *Sin'at yisrael le'doroteha*, edited by Shmuel Almog. Jerusalem: Shazar Center, 1980.

———. "Ha'kehila ha'yehudit be'maroqo ba'meia ha-18." Ph.D. diss., Hebrew University, 1981.

Bashan, Eliezer. "Rabbi eliyahu hazan, raban shel tripoli ve'alexandria, ve'yahaso la'haskala." Pp. 410–481 in *Hagut ivrit be'arsot ha'islam*, edited by Menahem Zohari et al. Jerusalem: Berit Ivrit Olamit, 1982.

Ben-Ami, Issachar. *Ha'arasat ha'qedoshim be'qerev yehudey maroqo.* Jerusalem: Magnes Press, 1984.

Ben-Malka, Ya'aqov. *Ner ma'aravi.* 3 vols. Jerusalem: 1932–1935.

Ben-Naim, Yoseif. *Malkhey rabanan.* Jerusalem: 1931.

Ben-Shetrit, Hayim. *Melel le'avraham.* Fez: 1963.

Bentov, Hayim. "Umanim u'va'aley melakha be'fas." *Sefunot* 10 (1966): 413–444.

―――. "Mishpahat ha'leivy-ibn-yuly." *Mi'mizrah u'mi'ma'arav* 2 (1980): 131–158.

―――. "Ha'toshavim be'fas min ha'meia ha-16." *Mi'mizrah u'mi'ma'arav* 5 (1986): 79–108.

Ben-Walid, Yishaq. *Va'yomer yishaq.* 2 vols. Leghorn: 1855.

Berdugo, Maimon. *Lev meivin.* Meknes: 1941.

Berdugo, Mordekhay. *Divrey mordekhay.* Meknes: 1947.

Berdugo, Moshe. *Divrey moshe.* Meknes: 1947.

Berdugo, Petahya. *Nofet sufim.* Casablanca: 1938.

Berdugo, Refael. *Mishpatim yesharim.* Cracow: 1891.

―――. *Mey menuhot.* 2 vols. Jerusalem (vol. 1), Djerba (vol. 2): 1905–1942.

Berdugo, Ya'aqov. *Shufrey de'ya'aqov.* Jerusalem: 1910.

Berdugo, Yoseif, I. *Kutonet yoseif.* 3 vols. Tiberias (vol. 1), Casablanca (vol. 2), Meknes (vol. 3): 1922–1943.

―――. *Divrey yoseif.* Jerusalem: 1974.

Berdugo, Yoseif, II. *Shufrey de'yoseif.* Jerusalem: 1972.

Bowie, Cleland. "An Aspect of Muslim-Jewish Relations in Late 19th Century Morocco: A European Diplomatic View." *International Journal of Middle East Studies* 7 (1976): 3–19.

Brown, Kenneth. "Profile of a Nineteenth-Century Moroccan Scholar." Pp. 127–148 in *Scholars, Saints and Sufis,* edited by Nikki Keddie. Berkeley: University of California Press, 1972.

―――. *People of Salé: Tradition and Change in a Moroccan City, 1830–1930.* Manchester: Manchester University Press, 1976.

―――. "A Moroccan City and Its Jewish Quarter." Pp. 253–281 in *Studies in Judaism and Islam,* edited by Shlomo Morag et al. Jerusalem: Magnes Press, 1981.

―――. "The 'Curse' of Westermarck." *Ethnos* 47 (1982): 197–231.

Burke, Edmund. "The Morocan Ulama, 1860–1912: An Introduction." Pp. 93–125 in *Scholars, Saints and Sufis,* edited by Nikki Keddie. Berkeley: University of California Press, 1972.

―――. *Prelude to Protectorate in Morocco.* Chicago: University of Chicago Press, 1976.

Caton, Steven. "Power, Persuasion and Language: A Critique of the Segmentary Model in the Middle East." *International Journal of Middle East Studies* 19 (1987): 77–102.

Chetrit, Yoseif. "Nisaneha shel tenuat haskala ivrit be'maroqo be'sof ha'meia ha-19." *Mi'qedem u'mi'yam* 2 (1986): 129–168.

Chouraqui, André. *Marche vers l'occident: les juifs d'afrique du nord.* Paris: Presses Universitaires de France, 1952.

Combs-Schilling, Elaine. "Family and Friend in a Moroccan Boom Town: The Segmentary Debate Reconsidered." *American Ethnologist* 12 (1985): 659–675.

Corcos, David. *Studies in the History of the Jews in Morocco.* Jerusalem: Rubin Mass, 1976.

Deshen, Shlomo. *Immigrant Voters in Israel: Parties and Congregations in a Local Election Campaign.* Manchester: Manchester University Press, 1970.

————. "Ethnicity and Citizenship in the Ritual of an Israeli Synagogue." *Southwestern Journal of Anthropology* 28 (1972): 69–82.

————. "Israeli Judaism: Introduction to the Major Patterns." *International Journal of Middle East Studies* 9 (1978): 141–169.

————. "The Social Structure of the Jewish Community in Djerba and Southern Tunisia." Pp. 123–135 in *Jewish Societies in the Middle-East,* edited by S. Deshen and W. Zenner. Wahington, D.C.: University Press of America, 1982.

————. *Sibbur vi'yehidim be'maroqo.* Tel Aviv: Misrad ha'bitahon, 1983.

Deshen, Shlomo, and Moshe Shokeid. *The Predicament of Homecoming: Cultural and Social Life of North African Immigrants in Israel.* Ithaca: Cornell University Press, 1974.

Deshen, Shlomo, and Walter Zenner, eds. *Jewish Societies in the Middle-East: Community, Culture and Authority.* Washington, D.C.: University Press of America, 1982.

Deverdun, Gaston. *Marrakesh: dès origines à 1912.* 2 vols. Rabat: 1959–1966.

Douglas, Mary. *Purity and Danger.* Harmondsworth: Penguin, 1966.

Eickelman, Dale. "Is There an Islamic City? The Making of a Moroccan Quarter in a Moroccan Town." *International Journal of Middle East Studies* 5 (1974): 274–294.

————. *Moroccan Islam: Tradition and Society in a Pilgrimage Center.* Austin: University of Texas Press, 1976.

————. *The Middle East: An Anthropological Approach.* Englewood Cliffs, N.J.: Prentice-Hall, 1981.

————. "Religion and Trade in Western Morocco." *Research in Economic Anthropology* 5 (1983): 335–348.

————. *Knowledge and Power in Morocco: The Education of a 20th Century Notable.* Princeton: Princeton University Press, 1985a.

————. "New Directions in Interpreting North-African Society." Pp. 279–289 in *Connaissances du Maghreb,* edited by J. C. Vatin et al. Paris: Centre National de la Recherche Scientifique, 1985b.

Eisenstadt, Shmuel N. *The Political Systems of Empires.* Glencoe, Ill.: Free Press, 1963.

Elbaum, Avraham. "Ha'eida ha'yehudit be'fas ba'meiot ha-17-18." Master's thesis, Bar-Ilan University, 1972.

Elbaz, Amram. *Hayey amram.* Meknes: 1949.

Elbaz, Refael Moshe. *Halakha le'moshe.* Jerusalem: 1901.

Elkhreif, Binyamin. *Gevul binyamin.* Casablanca: 1956.

Elmaleh, Yoseif. *Toqpo shel yoseif.* 2 vols. Leghorn: 1823–1855.

Evans-Pritchard, Edward. *The Sanusi of Cyrenaica.* Oxford: Clarendon Press, 1949.

Friedman, Yohannan. "Islam is superior . . ." *Jerusalem Quarterly* 11 (1979): 34–42.

Gaguine, Hayim. *Etz haim.* Edited by Moche Amar. Ramat Gan: Bar-Ilan University Press, 1987.

Geertz, Clifford. *Islam Observed.* Chicago: University of Chicago Press, 1968.

Geertz, Clifford, Hildred Geertz, and Lawrence Rosen. *Meaning and Order in Moroccan Society: Three Essays in Cultural Analysis.* Cambridge: Cambridge University Press, 1979.

Gellner, Ernest. *Saints of the Atlas*. London: Routledge and Kegan Paul, 1969.

Gellner, Ernest, and Charles Micaud, eds. *Arabs and Berbers: From Tribe to Nation in North-Africa*. London: Duckworth, 1973.

Gerber, Jane. *Jewish Society in Fez: 1465–1700*. Leiden: Brill, 1980.

Glazer, Mark. "The Dowry as Capital Accumulation among the Sephardic Jews of Istanbul, Turkey." *International Journal of Middle Eastern Studies* 10 (1979): 373–380.

Goitein, Shlomo D. *Studies in Islamic History and Institutions*. Leiden: Brill, 1966.

———. *A Mediterranean Society*. 4 vols. Berkeley: University of California Press, 1967–1983.

———, ed. *Religion in a Religious Age*. New York: Ktav, 1974.

Goldberg, Harvey E. "The Mimuna and Minority Status of Moroccan Jews." *Ethnology* 17 (1978): 75–87.

Haas, Peter. "The Modern Study of Responsa." Pp. 35–71 in *Approaches to Judaism in Mediaeval Times*, vol. 2, edited by David R. Blumenthal. Chico, Calif.: Scholars Press, 1985.

Harris, Walter. *Morocco That Was*. Edinburgh: Blackwood, 1921.

Hart, David. *The Ait 'Atta of Southern Morocco: Daily Life and Recent History*. Cambridge: Menas Press, 1984.

Heilman, Samuel. *Synagogue Life*. Chicago: University of Chicago Press, 1976.

Hirschberg, Hayim Z. "Ha'mellah: ha'rova' ha'yehudi be'maroqo." *Eres-Yisrael* 4 (1956): 225–230.

———. *A History of the Jews in North Africa*. Vol. 2. Leiden: Brill, 1981.

Ibn-Danan, Shlomo. *Asher li'shelomo*. Jerusalem: 1906.

Ibn-Danan, Yishaq. *Le'yishaq reiah*. Leghorn: 1902.

Ibn-Sur, Ya'aqov. *Mishpat u'sedaqa be'ya'aqov*. 2 vols. Alexandria: 1894–1903.

Jamous, Raymond. *Honneur et baraka: les structures sociales traditionelles dans le Rif*. Cambridge: Cambridge University Press, 1981.

Katz, Jacob. "Al halakha u'derush ki'meqorot historiyim." *Tarbiz* 30 (1960): 62–68.

———. *Tradition and Crisis: Jewish Society at the End of the Middle Ages*. New York: Free Press, 1961a.

———. *Exclusiveness and Tolerance: Studies in Jewish-Gentile Relations in Mediaeval and Modern Times*. Oxford: Oxford University Press, 1961b.

———. "Rabbinical Authority and Authorization in the Middle Ages." Pp. 41–56 in *Studies in Mediaeval Jewish History and Literature*, edited by Isadore Twersky, Cambridge, Mass.: Harvard University Press, 1979.

Kenbib, Mohammed. "Structures sociales et protections étrangères au Maroc au XIXe siècle." *Hespéris-Tamuda* 22 (1984): 79–101.

Khalfon, Ya'aqov. *Mishpatim sadiqim*. 3 vols. Jerusalem: 1932–1935.

Kirshenblatt-Gimblett, Barbara. "The Shtetl Model." In *Ashkenaz*. Bloomington: Indiana University Press (forthcoming).

Laskier, Michael. *The Alliance Israélite Universelle and the Jewish Communities of Morocco, 1862–1962*. Albany, N.Y.: SUNY Press, 1983.

Le Tourneau, Roger. *La vie quotidienne à Fez avant 1900*. Paris: Hachette, 1965.

Lewis, Bernard. *The Jews of Islam*. Princeton: Princeton University Press, 1984.

Loeb, Lawrence. "Prestige and Piety in the Iranian Synagogue." *Anthropological Quarterly* 51 (1978): 155–161.

Marcus, Ivan. *Piety and Society: The Jewish Pietists of Mediaeval Germany.* Leiden: Brill, 1981.

Mernissi, Fatima. *Beyond the Veil: Male-Female Dynamics in a Modern Muslim Society.* New York: Schenkman, 1975.

Meshash, Hayim. *Nishmat hayim.* Meknes: 1949.

Meshash, Yoseif. *Osar ha'mikhtavim.* 2 vols. Jerusalem: 1970.

Meyers, Allan F. "Power and Charisma: The Sultans of Morocco as Amir al-Mu'minim." Paper presented at the Conference on Modern Morocco, University of Durham, England, 1977.

———. "Patronage and Protection: The Status of Jews in Precolonial Morocco." Pp. 85–104 in *Jewish Societies in the Middle East,* edited by Shlomo Deshen and Walter Zenner. Washington, D.C.: University Press of America, 1982.

Miège, Jean-Louis. "La bourgeoisie juive du Maroc au 19e siècle: rupture ou continuité." Pp. 25–36 in *Judaïsme d'Afrique du Nord aux 19e–20e siècles,* edited by Michel Abitbol. Jerusalem: Ben-Zvi Institute, 1980.

Moghrabi, Avraham. *Ma'aseh nissim.* Jerusalem: 1968.

Monsoniego, Yedidia. *Divrey emet.* Fez: 1952.

Montbard, John. *Among the Moors: Sketches of Oriental Life.* London: 1894.

Noy, Dov. *Jewish Folktales from Morocco.* Jerusalem: World Zionist Organization, 1964.

Ovadia, David. *Qehilat Sefrou.* 4 vols. Jerusalem: 1975–1985.

———. *Fas va'hakhameha.* 2 vols. Jerusalem: 1979.

Ovadia, Yeshu'a, S. H. *Torah ve'hayim.* Jerusalem: 1972.

Perlmann, Moshe. "The Medieval Polemics between Islam and Judaism." Pp. 103–138 in *Religion in a Religious Age,* edited by S. D. Goitein. New York: Ktav, 1974.

Quriat, Avraham. *Zekhut avot.* Pisa: 1817.

Rosen, Lawrence. "Muslim-Jewish Relations in a Moroccan City." *International Journal of Middle East Studies* 4 (1972): 435–449.

———. *Bargaining for Reality: The Construction of Social Relations in a Muslim Community.* Chicago: University of Chicago Press, 1984.

Schroeter, Daniel. "The Jews of Essaouira (Mogador) and the Trade of Southern Morocco." Pp. 365–390 in *Communautés juives des marges sahariennes du Maghreb,* edited by M. Abitbol. Jerusalem: Ben-Zvi Institute, 1982.

———. "The Politics of Reform in Morocco: The Writings of Yishaq ben Ya'ish Halewi in Ha'sefirah (1891)." Paper presented at the Second International Congress for the Study of Sephardi and Oriental Jewry, Jerusalem, 1984a.

———. "Merchants and Pedlars of Essaouira: A Social History of a Moroccan Trading Town (1844–1886)." Ph.D. diss., Manchester University, 1984b.

———. "Trade as a Mediator in Muslim-Jewish Relations: Southwestern Morocco in the 19th Century." Unpublished paper, n.d.

Seroussi, Edwin. "Shinui ve'hemshekhiut be'shirat ha'baqashot shel yehudey maroqo." *Pe'amim* 19 (1984): 113–129.

Sharot, Stephen. *Messianism, Mysticism and Magic: A Sociological Analysis of Jewish Religious Movements.* Chapel Hill: University of North Carolina Press, 1982.

Shokeid, Moshe. "The Decline of Personal Endowment of Atlas Mountains Religious Leaders." *Anthropological Quarterly* 52 (1979): 186–197.

———. "The Regulation of Aggression in Daily Life: Aggressive Relationships among Moroccan Immigrants in Israel." *Ethnology* 21 (1982): 271–281.

———. *The Dual Heritage: Immigrants from the Atlas Mountains in an Israeli Village.* Manchester: Manchester University Press, 1971 (augmented ed., Transaction Books, 1985).

Stahl, Avraham. " 'Al sifrey hakhmey maroqo." *Yad laqoreh* 18 (1979a): 143–149.

———. "Ritualistic Reading among Oriental Jews." *Anthropological Quarterly* 52 (1979b): 115–120.

———. "Shivhey rabbi ya'aqov abihsera." *Mi'mizrah u'mi'ma'arav* 2 (1980): 159–170.

Stillman, Norman. "Muslims and Jews in Morocco." *Jerusalem Quarterly* 5 (1977): 74–83.

———. "The Moroccan Jewish Experience: A Revisionist View." *Jerusalem Quarterly* 9 (1978): 111–123.

———. "Aspects of Jewish Life in Islamic Spain." Pp. 51–84 in *Aspects of Jewish Culture in the Middle Ages,* edited by P. E. Szarmach. Albany: State University of New York Press, 1979a.

———. *Jews in Arab Lands: A History and Source Book.* Philadelphia: Jewish Publication Society, 1979b.

———. "Saddiq and Marabout in Morocco." Pp. 489–500 in *The Sephardic and Oriental Jewish Heritage,* edited by Issakhar Ben-Ami. Jerusalem: Magnes Press, 1982.

Toledano, Hayim. *Hoq u'mishpat.* Fez: 1931.

Toledano, Moshe. *Ha'shamayim ha'hadashim.* Casablanca: 1939.

Tuito, Elazar. "Ha'hinukh ha'yehudi be'maroqo ba'meia ha-18." *Ha'hinukh* 33 (1982): 137–148.

Waterbury, John. "The coup manqué." Pp. 397–423 in *Arabs and Berbers,* edited by Ernest Gellner and Charles Micaud. London: Duckworth, 1973.

Weinryb, Bernard D. "Responsa as a Source for History: Methodological Problems." Pp. 399–416 in *Essays presented to Chief Rabbi Israel Brodie,* edited by H. J. Zimmels and J. Rabbinowitz. London: Jews' College Publications, 1967.

Westermarck, Edward. *Ritual and Belief in Morocco.* 2 vols. London: Macmillan, 1926.

INDEX

Abihsera, Ya'aqov, 21, 24, 117
Abitbol, Michel, 126n.14
Abitbul, Sha'ul Yeshu'a, 43, 55, 56, 58–59, 75
Abitbul, Shlomo, 71, 73, 74, 95, 108, 133n.12
Abitbul family, 88
Abu-Lughod, Janet, 124
Adultery, 129n.5
Aged, 68
Aguna, 40, 63, 142n.1
'Alawi, 15–17
Alexandria, 10
Alliance Israélite Universelle, 7, 104; schools of, 7
Almohads, 13
Amar, Moche, x, 126n.11, 129n.1, 133n.5, 134n.15
Amar, Shmuel, 125n.6
Amir al-mu'minin, 15, 127n.3
Amzallag, Avraham, 135n.7
Ancestors, 113–114. *See also* Zekhut avot
Andalusia, 125n.8
Anqawe, Avraham, 41, 51, 52, 70, 87, 95, 126n.11
Anqawe, Refael, 105, 106, 110
Anthropology, Maghrebi, 2–4, 123–124
Apprenticeship, 43
'*Ar,* 21
Aragon, 125n.8
Archives. *See* documentary sources
Army, 16
Arusi, Rason, 129n.2
Ashkenazi, Avraham, 128n.11
Ashkenazic Jews, 3, 23, 74, 107, 115, 129n.2, 130n.6, 133nn.7, 8, and 12, 134n.18, 137n.9
Attal, Robert, xi, 9
Authorities, Muslim, 14, 28, 54–58, 71;

extortions of, 29, 62–63, 117
Azamour, 136n.14
Azulay, Hayim Y. D., 130n.4

Baer, Yitzhak, 6
Baqashot. See Hymns
Baraka, 14–15
Bar-Asher, Shalom, x, 126n.11, 128nn.9 and 13, 129n.1, 135n.8
Bar-Sheishet, Yishaq, 92
Bashan, Eliezer, x, 128n.10
Beggars, 40, 66, 129n.3
Beit-din. See Court
Beit-midrash. See Yeshiva
Ben-Adrat, Shlomo, 100
Ben-Ami, Issachar, x, 134n.15
Ben-Atar, Yehuda, 10, 134n.17
Ben-Malka, Ya'aqov, 28, 60, 68, 79, 82, 87, 91, 93, 97, 125n.7, 133n.5
Ben-Naim, Yoseif, 79, 134n.15
Ben-Shetrit, Hayim, 116
Ben-Walid, Yishaq, 49, 77, 80, 93, 117, 129n.1, 136nn.10 and 11, 138n.1
Bentov, Hayim, 37, 43, 99, 121, 129n.4, 137n.2
Berbers. *See* Tribesmen
Berdugo, Maimon, 48, 130n.5, 131n.10, 137n.9
Berdugo, Mordekhay, 28, 49, 120
Berdugo, Moshe, 98, 136n.15
Berdugo, Petahya, 25, 92, 97, 128n.13
Berdugo, Refael, 22, 43, 44, 48, 52, 92, 94, 97, 136n.14
Berdugo, Ya'aqov, 41, 54, 72, 90, 91, 95, 98, 105
Berdugo, Yoseif I, 28, 54, 60, 76–77, 80, 83, 84, 97, 98, 100, 110, 111, 133n.11, 134n.16

Berdugo, Yoseif II, 40, 89, 93, 96, 98, 135n.7
Berdugo family, 98
Bibas family, 135n.10
Birth, illegitimate, 116
Blad al-makhzan, 17, 19
Blad e-siba 17
Blessing, 104
Books, 86–87, 135n.3
Boujad, 35
Bowie, Cleland, 125n.6
Brown, Kenneth, 21, 125n.1, 127n.4
Bureaucracy, 16
Burglary. See Robbery
Burial society, 60
Burke, Edmund, 125n.1, 127nn.1, 4, and 7

Cairo, 4
Capitulation agreements, 7, 20, 44
Castille, 125n.8
Caton, Steven, 125n.1
Cemetery. See Graves
Charisma, 15, 18
Charity, 62–69, 92; administration of, 67; endowment of, 65–66; formalization of, 66–67; funds of, 79; officials of, 65
Chetrit, Yoseif, 7
Children, 50, 108, 135n.4
Chouraqui, André, 10, 31, 33, 104
Christian-Jewish relations, 5, 6, 18, 23–26
Church, 24
Clothes, maintenance of, 112
Colonialism. See Imperialism
Combs-Schilling, Elaine, 125n.1
Communities, administration of, 47; boundaries of, 124; committees of, 47, 63, 129n.1; finances of, 56; judicial autonomy in, 27–28; self-view of, 70
Corcos, David, 37, 129n.4
Court, Jewish, 28, 43, 47, 48, 50, 51, 53, 54, 75, 76, 79, 98, 116, 125n.6; appeal, 76, 77; Muslim, 28; quorum of, 75. See also Law
Cracow, 10
Craftsmen, 33–34, 37, 63–64; associations of, 43, 44
"Crise maraboutique," 14
Crowdedness, 87, 122, 137n.2
Crypto-Jews, 129n.4
Curses, 113, 132n.2

Dayan. See judge
Day of Atonement, 135n.7
Debate, interfaith, 24–25
Debdou, 135n.9
Defense of mellah, 20–21, 62
Defilement, 78–79
Deinstitutionalization, 120–121
Demnat, 20
Demography, 31–34, 105, 138n.2
Derasha. See Preaching
Deshen, Shlomo, ix, xi, 112, 125nn.2 and 4, 132n.2, 133nn.3, and 13, 134nn.1 and 15
Deverdun, Gaston, 31, 130n.5
Dhimmi, 18, 26, 36, 55, 127n.6
Disasters, 30, 128n.1
Divorce, 113, 129n.2, 130n.5; law of, 121; payments upon, 28
Documentary sources, ix, 8, 10–11, 53, 126n.13, 128n.13; loss of, 126n.12
Douglas, Mary, 138n.17
Dowry, 72, 114
Duran family, 101

Eastern Europe, Jews in, 86. See also Ashkenazic Jews
Education 42, 72–73, 133n.8; rabbinical, 74
Egypt, x
Eickelman, Dale, x, 2, 35, 36, 124, 125n.1, 127n.4, 128n.10
Eisenstadt, Shmuel N., 3
Elbaum, Avraham, 43
Elbaz, Amram, 56, 58, 82
Elbaz, Refael M., 25, 49, 66, 68, 76, 94, 95, 122, 135n.4
Elbaz family, 71
Elkhreif, Binyamin, 54, 96, 97, 98, 126n.12, 136n.13
Elmaleh, Yoseif, 49, 50, 52, 64, 97, 98, 115
Employees, 43
Enclosure in mellah, 20
Endogamy, 137n.3
Endowments, religious, 59
Eretz Yisrael. See Israel
Essaouira, 20, 30, 31, 32, 64, 128n.1, 136n.2
Ethnography, 3, 132n.4, 134n.1. See also Jewry, comparative study
Evans-Pritchard, Edward, 125n.1
Excommunication, 50, 51, 52, 83, 84

Familism, 52–53, 73, 117
Family, 63, 104–118, 129n.5; disputes in, 106–113; extended, 104, 113, 115, 116; ideal of, 104; nuclear, 115; property of, 114–115; size of, 105; taint of, 116; visiting among, 22, 23
Fez, 8, 13, 17, 23, 28, 31, 32, 33, 38, 39, 41, 42, 43, 54, 58, 63, 64, 67, 72, 73, 75, 76, 77, 78, 80, 81, 83, 87, 91, 94, 95, 99, 100, 115, 121, 125n.7, 126n.10, 129n.3, 130n.5, 132n.3, 133n.5; custom of, 98–102, 138n.1; occupations in, 37–39
Fieldwork, anthropological, ix, x, 135n.5, 138n.12
Fines 54
Food preparation, 111
Formalization, 47, 64, 80, 81
Fqih, 25, 128n.11
Friedman, Yohannan, 26

Gaguine, Hayim, 126n.9
Geertz, Clifford, 2, 35, 36, 123, 125n.1
Gellner, Ernest, 125n.1, 127n.1
Geniza, 3, 4, 125n.4
Gerber, Jane, 126n.13
Gibraltar, 92
Glazer, Mark, 115
Goitein, Shlomo D., x, 3, 4
Goldberg, Harvey, 22
Grace after meals. See Prayer
Graves, 99; of sages, 83; visiting, 22, 83. See also Saint veneration

Haas, Peter, 11
Hagiography, 24, 85
Hakham. See Sages
Hakhamim reshumim, 132n.1
Halakha, 9, 84, 101. See also Law
Harka, 16–18
Harris, Walter, 17
Hart, David, 127n.8
Hasidei ashkenaz, 6
Hassidism, 6, 134n.18
Hazaka, 131n.13, 132n.2, 136n.11
Head covering, 24
Hebron, 132n.3
Heilman, Samuel, 135n.1
Hevrat hesgeir, 87. See also Yeshiva
Hirschberg, Hayim Z., 10, 11, 58, 127n.7
History, study, 2; Jewish, 4–12

Holiness, 14
Holy days, 88–89
Homosexuality, 51
Honor, 19
"Honor and shame," 36–37
Hosting, 65, 68, 103
"Host societies," 5–6
Housing, 105
Humiliation of Jews, 131n.8
Hymns, 25, 88, 135n.7

Ibn-Danan, Shlomo, 116, 121
Ibn-Danan, Yishaq, 45, 49, 82
Ibn-Danan chronicles, 38
Ibn-Danan family, 8, 72
Ibn-Sur, Ya'aqov, 23, 28, 29, 30, 38, 43, 51, 53, 54, 57, 63, 64, 68, 75, 79, 93, 96, 106, 108, 111, 116, 126n.12, 128n.1, 129nn.1 and 5, 130nn.5 and 7, 131n.9, 132n.3, 133n.5, 135nn.3 and 9, 136nn.11 and 15
Imam, 25
Imperialism, 7, 17, 20, 44
Imprisonment, 54, 80, 130n.5, 131n.10; release from, 117
Individualism, 2, 47–48, 102–103
Individuals, 47, 129n.1; gatherings of, 49, 51
Inequity, 57, 63
Informer, 38
Inheritance, 115–116
Insult. See Violence, verbal
Insurgence. See Rebellion
Interaction, personal, 16
Iraq, Jews in, 5
Islam, 13, 15, 18–19, 92, 127n.2, 138n.17; conversion to, 26–27, 29, 37–38, 63, 116, 129n.4; cursing of, 56; "Islamic city," 120–124; Jewish view of, 23–26; Moroccan, 2, 3; view of Jewry, 18, 26
Ismail ibn-al-Sharif, 127n.3
Israel, 3, 65, 112, 129n.2, 133n.7; emigrants in, x, 3, 66, 111, 113, 132n.4, 133n.9, 135n.5, 137n.8, 138n.12; emissaries from, 65, 67, 130n.6, 132n.3
Italy, x

Jamous, Raymond, 21, 37, 127n.1
Jerusalem, 67, 128n.10
Jewry, comparative study, 4–5, 112, 115, 117, 133nn.6–8.

Judeo-Maghrebi studies, 3
Judge 47, 76–77; appointment of, 71–75,
  income of, 79
Jurisdiction, 27, 44

Katz, Jacob, 2, 3, 11, 23, 133nn.7 and 12
Kenbib, Mohammed, 125n.6.
Ketuba, 72, 114–115
Khalfon, Ya'aqov, 49, 129n.1
King Hassan, 127n.5
Kirshenblatt-Gimblett, Barbara, 125n.3

Language, 128n.10
Laskier, Michael, 7, 31
Law, lay, 53–55, 130nn.4 and 7; religious,
  16, 18, 23, 53–55; equality before, 52;
  abidance by, 52. See also Sages
Leghorn, 10
Legislation, 47, 49–51
Legitimization, 15, 16; religious, 127n.3;
  of appointments, 73; of legislation, 70
Le Tourneau, Roger, 31, 37
Lewis, Bernard, 131n.8
Literati, 7
Litigation, 27, 97. See also Sages
Local-patriotism, 41, 42
Loeb, Lawrence, 135n.1
Luck, 56

Ma'amad. See Communities, administration
  of
Maimonides, 72, 137n.6
Malaga, 24
Malka, Moshe, 133n.10
Marabout, 14–16, 84, 127n.4
Marcus, Ivan, 6
Marrakesh, 8, 17, 20, 30–32, 125n.7,
  129n.4, 130n.5; custom of, 98–102,
  138n.1
Marriage, 51–52, 107, 115; arrangement
  of, 23, 107, 128n.10; engagement to,
  38, 108, 116; gifts at, 114
Matrilineality, 97, 138n.16
Matrilocality, 110, 137n.9
Mazagan, 31
Megorashim. See Sephardim
Meknes, 8, 17, 22, 31, 35, 39, 47, 54,
  57, 58, 60, 66, 71, 76, 77, 83, 84, 87,
  91, 93, 94, 97, 99–101, 105, 106,
  125n.6, 129nn.1 and 3, 130n.5,
  131n.10, 133nn.5 and 11, 135n.4;

sages of, 134n.15; occupations in, 33–
  34
Merchants, 34–36, 63–64; associations of,
  44
Mernissi, Fatima, 117
Meshash, Hayim, 66, 83, 105, 126n.12,
  129n.1, 135n.4
Meshash, Yoseif, 24, 107
Methodology, ix, x, 4, 133n.14, 136n.13
Meyers, Allan, 123, 127n.3
Micaud, Charles, 127n.1
Miège, Jean-Louis, 125n.6
Mimuna, 22
Miqve, 50, 112, 136n.11
Misva, 67, 132n.3; of women, 110; selling
  of, 67
Models, 4, 123, 125n.3
Mogador. See Essaouira
Moghrabi, Avraham, 24, 134n.15
Mohammed ibn-Abd'allah, 127n.3
Monsoniego, Yedidia, 50, 82, 92, 97, 100
Montbard, John, 137n.2
Mosque-universities, 14, 18
Mulay Hasan, 17, 18
Muslim-Jewish relations, 18, 19, 22–24,
  55, 116, 132n.2. See also Islam

Nagid, 47, 53–61, 73, 130n.5, 131nn.9–
  12, 133n.5; appointment of, 57–60;
  harm to, 58; reimbursement of, 56–61,
  131n.12
Names, 14, 38, 126n.10
Noy, Dov, 85, 134n.15

Oath, 60, 63, 77, 109. See also 'Ar
Occupations, 36; in Boujad, 35; in Mek-
  nees, 33–34; in Sefrou, 33–35; in Fez,
  37, 39
Officials, salary of, 48, 120
Ovadia, David, x, 25, 110, 136n.11
Ovadia, Yeshu'a, 88, 135n.4

Parnas, 47
Patrilocality, 105, 108, 110
Patron-client relations, 21–22, 27, 28, 53,
  55, 123–124, 127n.8, 128nn.10 and
  15, 130n.5
Peddlers, 20, 32, 33–34, 35, 37, 39, 88–
  89; assaulted, 21; killed, 40; protected,
  20–21
Periodization, 4–10
Perlmann, Moshe, 25

Persecution of Jews, 8, 37, 38
Philosophy, 6
Pisa, x, 10
Piyutim. See Hymns
Play on words, 41, 128n.12
Poetry, 7
Poland, x, 65
Polemics, religious, 25
Poll-tax, 62, 130n.8
Polygamy, 30, 41, 111, 121, 129n.2
Poor, 65, 68, 90, 130n.6; support of, 60
Popular religion, 50, 120
Population expansion, 31–32, 102
Potentates. See Authorities, Muslim
"Power of the weak," 127–128n.9
Prayer, 39, 88, 89, 92, 136n.12; with
   Muslims, 128n.9
Preaching, 42, 86
Priest, Catholic, 24
Printing, x, 9, 10, 126n.12
Privacy, 105, 111
Promiscuity, 54
Property, landed, 59, 131n.13
Public announcements, 49–50
Punishment, 55, 84, 110, 130n.6

Qabala, 81
Quriat, Avraham, 98, 125n.7

Rabat, 20, 50, 52, 129n.4, 132n.2
Rebellion, 15, 20, 127n.5, 128n.15
Reconquista, 127n.2
Rentals, 122
Responsa, ix; pagination of, xiii; publica-
   tion, x, xiii, 10; critical use of, 11. See
   also Documentary sources
Revitalization movements, 13, 127n.2
Rhineland, 6
Rights of Jews, 46
Robbery, 21, 40, 54, 83
Rosen, Lawrence, 21, 31, 34, 35, 123,
   125n.1

Sabbath, 40, 49, 86, 88, 89, 114, 137n.7
Sabbatianism, 136n.16
Sages, ix, 47, 50–59, 63, 65, 70–103,
   112, 126n.9, 131n.12, 132n.1,
   135n.9, 137n.10; appointment of, 74–
   75, 81; creativity of, 10; disputes of,
   79, 90; duties of, 86, 90; families of, 8,
   71–72, 82, 133n.6, 137n.3; ideal of,

79, 84, 85; income of, 71, 78–80, 88–
   90, 122; respect for, 82, 83, 134n.16;
   taxation of, 68; urban bias, 39–41
Saint veneration, 84–85, 134nn.15, 17,
   and 18. See *also* Graves, visiting
Salé, 20, 51
Sanctions. See Punishment
Sarfati, Eliyahu, 73–75, 94
School, 7, 87, 95
Schroeter, Daniel, 7, 20, 31, 64, 125n.6,
   128n.1, 134n.15, 137n.2, 138n.2
Sefrou, x, 21, 22, 28, 31, 32, 39, 41, 42,
   49, 51, 53, 55, 58, 60, 63, 66, 73, 75–
   80, 83, 84, 87, 88, 91, 93, 95, 108,
   110, 116, 120, 129nn.1 and 3,
   131nn.11 and 12, 133n.12, 135nn.4
   and 6, 136n.11; occupations in, 34–35
Seifer Ha'taqanot, 9, 10, 23, 25, 46, 65,
   70, 81, 121, 126n.11, 130n.5, 136n.13
Seifer tashbeis, 101
Semikha. See Sages, appointment of
Sephardim, 8, 119, 121, 125n.7, 126n.9;
   custom of, 8, 119–120; disapora of,
   126n.10; sages of, 8, 37; Turkish, 115
Serara, 71, 72, 80, 89, 90, 96, 97, 100.
   See *also* Sages
Seroussi, Edwin, 135n.7
"Seven elders," 47, 49, 129n.1
Sexuality, 50, 112–113
Sharot, Stephen, 6, 128n.14
Sherira Gaon, 84
Shoheit, 47, 48, 80, 129n.1
Shokeid, Moshe, x, 3, 21, 111, 113,
   125n.4, 132n.4, 133n.9, 134n.15,
   135n.1
Social control, 41, 44–45
Socializing, 109–110, 137n.7
Social relationships, 47, 123–124
Spain, 128n.14
Stahl, Avraham, 24, 87, 126n.12,
   134n.15
Stillman, Norman, xi, 10, 19, 20, 25, 26,
   84, 123
Sultan, 15–20, 22
Synagogue, 23, 67, 86–103, 110, 114,
   126n.10, 128n.15, 135n.2; private, 49,
   51, 78–79, 89, 90–91, 94–95,
   136n.15; public, 78, 89–90, 94, 98,
   120, 135n.10; as capital, 97; availability
   of, 95; autonomy of, 96; charity in, 66;
   cantor of, 23; decorum and maintenance,
   90, 88, 92; honors in, 51; regulations,

Synagogue (*continued*)
50; splitting of, 94, 136n.14; women in, 137n.8

Tafilalt, 15, 21, 22, 23, 125n.7
Taharat hamishpaha, 112. *See also* Women, impurity of
Tangier, 7, 9, 31, 106
Taqanot. See Legislation
Taxes, 16, 23–24, 28, 46, 52, 53, 55, 57, 62–69; at celebrations, 65; assessment, 62–63; collection of, 64; direct, 62–64; evasion of, 47, 131n.9, 132n.2; exemption from, 60, 68; farming, 64; indirect, 59–60, 62, 64; irregular, 62–63; on meat, 65
Teachers, 87, 94, 107, 135n.4
Tetuan, 7, 20, 49, 60, 77, 91, 92, 93, 129n.1, 135nn.4 and 10, 138n.1
Theft. *See* Robbery
Theory, 1–3
Toledano, Hayim, 23, 28, 30–31, 57, 65
Toledano, Moshe, 28, 38, 40, 43, 54, 79, 82, 91, 101, 137n.10, 138n.16
Toledano, Ya'aqov, 101
Toledano family, 72
Torah, reading, 30, 114; study, 70, 86, 87, 137n.9
Toshavim, 8, 99, 119, 126n.9; customs of, 8. *See also* Marrakesh, custom of
Travelers, 53, 65, 105. *See also* Beggars; Peddlers
Treasury of community, 59–60
Tribesmen, 13, 14, 15, 17, 20, 36, 40, 127n.8

Tuito, Elazar, 135n.2
Tunisia, Jews in, 4, 112, 133n.12

Udovitch, A. L., 125n.4
Ulama, 14, 16, 18, 22, 26, 37, 38, 127n.4
Union, labor, 43

Va'ad, 133n.9
Verbosity, 117
Violence, 113; domestic, 107; verbal 84, 110, 134n.16
Visiting, 109, 110, 137n.7. *See also* Graves

Wanderers. *See* Beggars; Peddlers; Travelers
Waterbury, John, 127n.5
Weber, Max, 2
Weinryb, Bernard, 11
Westermarck, Edward, 21
Women, 50, 82, 83; aged, 110; agnates of, 111, 113, 138n.11; in synagogue, 110; impurity of, 79, 110, 118, 138n.17; married, 106–114, 138n.11; Muslim, 36; residence of married, 40–41; resources of, 111; seclusion of, 109–110; status of, 111; widowed, 115
Writing, 106, 109, 137n.6

Yahid. See Individuals
Yemen, 86, 129n.2, 133n.6; Jews in, 5
Yeshiva 70, 88, 135n.6

Zekhut avot, 72, 84
Zenner, Walter, xi, 125n.2
Zohar reading, 87, 135n.5